DYLAN PARKER

Virtual Reality and Human Experience: Redefining Reality

How VR and AR are Changing Our World

Copyright © 2024 by Dylan Parker

All rights reserved. No part of this publication may be reproduced, stored or transmitted in any form or by any means, electronic, mechanical, photocopying, recording, scanning, or otherwise without written permission from the publisher. It is illegal to copy this book, post it to a website, or distribute it by any other means without permission.

Dylan Parker asserts the moral right to be identified as the author of this work.

Dylan Parker has no responsibility for the persistence or accuracy of URLs for external or third-party Internet Websites referred to in this publication and does not guarantee that any content on such Websites is, or will remain, accurate or appropriate.

Designations used by companies to distinguish their products are often claimed as trademarks. All brand names and product names used in this book and on its cover are trade names, service marks, trademarks and registered trademarks of their respective owners. The publishers and the book are not associated with any product or vendor mentioned in this book. None of the companies referenced within the book have endorsed the book.

First edition

This book was professionally typeset on Reedsy.
Find out more at reedsy.com

Contents

1. Introduction: The Emergence of Virtual Reality — 1
2. The Evolution of Entertainment — 10
3. Educational Frontiers — 23
4. Therapeutic Applications — 34
5. Social Interaction and Virtual Communities — 45
6. Redefining Reality — 57
7. Ethical and Societal Implications — 70
8. Future Directions and Innovations — 82
9. Conclusion: Embracing the Virtual Frontier — 94
10. Appendix — 97

1

Introduction: The Emergence of Virtual Reality

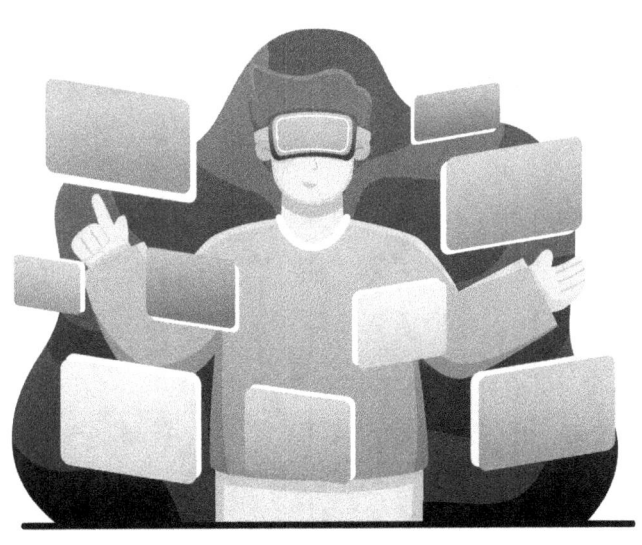

Historical Overview: From Sci-Fi Dreams to Real-World Innovation

Virtual reality may seem like a recent phenomenon, but its roots stretch back further than you might think. The concept of creating immersive, simulated environments has been a staple of science fiction for decades, capturing the imagination of writers and filmmakers alike. Who could forget the iconic scenes from movies like *The Matrix* or *Ready Player One* that painted vivid pictures of what virtual worlds might one day look like?

The journey from imagination to reality began in earnest in the mid-20th century. Early pioneers like Morton Heilig, who created the Sensorama in the 1960s, laid the groundwork for VR by developing one of the first machines designed to immerse users in a multi-sensory environment. In the decades that followed, research and development continued, often within the realms of academia and military training, where the potential for virtual simulations was eagerly explored.

1. The Sensorama and Early Experiments

Morton Heilig's Sensorama was a revolutionary device that combined stereoscopic 3D images, sound, vibrations, and even smells to create an immersive experience. Though it was ahead of its time, the Sensorama was never commercially successful. However, it laid the foundation for future developments in VR technology.

During the 1960s and 1970s, other inventors and researchers began exploring similar concepts. Ivan Sutherland and his student Bob Sproull created the first head-mounted display (HMD) system, known as "The

Sword of Damocles." This device was rudimentary and required users to be tethered to a computer, but it demonstrated the potential of HMDs for immersive experiences.

2. Military and Academic Research

Throughout the 1980s and 1990s, VR technology continued to evolve, driven by military and academic research. The military saw the potential of VR for training simulations, allowing soldiers to practise maneuvers and tactics in a controlled, virtual environment. This period saw the development of sophisticated flight simulators and other training systems that utilized VR to enhance realism and effectiveness.

Academic institutions also played a significant role in advancing VR technology. Researchers at institutions like the Massachusetts Institute of Technology (MIT) and Stanford University explored the applications of VR in various fields, from psychology to architecture. These efforts helped refine the technology and broaden its potential uses.

3. Commercialization and Popularization

The 1990s marked a turning point in the commercialization of VR. Companies like VPL Research, founded by Jaron Lanier, began developing VR hardware and software for consumer and industrial markets. Lanier is credited with popularizing the term "virtual reality" and was a key figure in promoting the technology's potential.

Despite these advancements, early VR systems were expensive and cumbersome, limiting their appeal to a niche market. It wasn't until the early 2010s that VR began to gain mainstream traction, thanks to significant improvements in technology and reductions in cost.

4. The Modern Era of VR

The launch of the Oculus Rift Kickstarter campaign in 2012 marked the beginning of the modern era of VR. Oculus VR, founded by Palmer Luckey, aimed to create an affordable and high-quality VR headset for consumers. The campaign was a massive success, raising nearly $2.5 million and sparking renewed interest in VR technology.

In 2014, Facebook acquired Oculus VR for $2 billion, signaling a major investment in the future of VR. This acquisition brought significant resources and attention to the development of VR technology, accelerating its progress.

Other major technology companies soon followed suit. HTC, in partnership with Valve, released the HTC Vive in 2016, offering room-scale VR experiences. Sony launched the PlayStation VR, bringing VR to the console gaming market. These developments, combined with advances in smartphone-based VR systems like Google Cardboard and Samsung Gear VR, made VR more accessible to the general public.

Current Landscape: Virtual Reality Today

Fast forward to today, and VR has grown from its niche origins into a mainstream phenomenon. What was once the stuff of science fiction is now a vibrant industry with applications spanning entertainment, education, therapy, and social interaction. Modern VR headsets, like the Oculus Rift, HTC Vive, and PlayStation VR, offer immersive experiences that were unimaginable just a few years ago. These devices, combined with powerful software, allow users to step into entirely new worlds with a level of realism and interactivity that continues to improve.

1. Consumer VR: Gaming and Beyond

Gaming remains one of the most popular applications of VR technology. Games like *Beat Saber*, *Half-Life: Alyx*, and *The Walking Dead: Saints & Sinners* showcase the immersive potential of VR, offering experiences that are engaging and interactive in ways that traditional gaming cannot match.

But VR is not limited to gaming. Applications in education, such as *Google Expeditions*, allow students to take virtual field trips to historical sites, explore the human body, or travel to outer space. In the medical field, VR is used for surgical training, pain management, and therapy for conditions like PTSD and anxiety.

2. Enterprise and Industrial Applications

Beyond consumer applications, VR is making significant inroads in enterprise and industrial sectors. Companies use VR for employee training, virtual prototyping, and design collaboration. In architecture and construction, VR allows stakeholders to visualize and interact with building designs before construction begins, reducing errors and improving efficiency.

In the automotive industry, manufacturers like Ford and BMW use VR to design and test vehicles, allowing engineers to identify and address potential issues early in the development process. These applications demonstrate the versatility and value of VR in various professional contexts.

3. Social VR: Connecting People in Virtual Spaces

Social VR platforms, such as *VRChat, AltspaceVR,* and *Rec Room,* are creating new ways for people to connect and interact. In these virtual spaces, users can create avatars, explore environments, and engage in activities with others from around the world. These platforms offer a sense of presence and community that transcends physical distance, fostering new forms of social interaction.

For example, *AltspaceVR* hosts virtual events, such as concerts, comedy shows, and meetups, where users can participate and interact in real-time. These experiences provide a glimpse into the future of social interaction, where virtual presence complements and enhances real-world connections.

4. Augmented Reality: Enhancing the Real World

While VR creates entirely new worlds, AR enhances our existing reality by overlaying digital information onto the physical environment. AR applications like *Pokémon GO* and *Microsoft HoloLens* demonstrate the potential of this technology to blend the digital and physical worlds seamlessly.

INTRODUCTION: THE EMERGENCE OF VIRTUAL REALITY

AR is being used in various industries, from retail and marketing to healthcare and education. For instance, AR can enhance shopping experiences by allowing customers to visualize products in their homes before purchasing or provide real-time information and navigation in complex environments like airports and hospitals.

The Promise of Future Innovations

As we look to the future, the potential of VR and AR is vast and exciting. Continuous advancements in technology will lead to even more immersive and accessible experiences, transforming how we work, play, and interact.

1. Advancements in Hardware

Future VR and AR hardware will be lighter, more comfortable, and more powerful. Improvements in display technology will provide higher resolution and wider field of view, while advancements in haptic feedback will enable more realistic tactile experiences. Wireless and standalone headsets will become more prevalent, offering greater freedom of movement and ease of use.

2. Integration with Artificial Intelligence

The integration of AI with VR and AR will unlock new possibilities for personalized and adaptive experiences. AI-driven characters and environments will respond dynamically to user interactions, creating more engaging and realistic virtual worlds. Machine learning algorithms will analyze user behavior to tailor content and recommendations, enhancing the overall experience.

3. Expanding Content and Applications

As the ecosystem of VR and AR content continues to grow, we will see more diverse and innovative applications. From virtual tourism and remote collaboration to therapeutic interventions and interactive storytelling, the possibilities are limited only by our imagination. The democratization of content creation tools will empower more creators to develop unique experiences, enriching the VR and AR landscapes.

4. Societal and Ethical Considerations

With the widespread adoption of VR and AR, it is crucial to address the societal and ethical implications of these technologies. Issues such as privacy, data security, accessibility, and the impact on mental health must be carefully considered. By fostering responsible innovation and promoting ethical guidelines, we can ensure that the benefits of VR and AR are realized while minimizing potential risks.

INTRODUCTION: THE EMERGENCE OF VIRTUAL REALITY

Conclusion: Embracing the Virtual Frontier

As we stand at the threshold of this exciting new frontier, it is clear that VR is not just a passing trend but a profound shift in how we perceive and interact with reality. In this book, we will explore the many ways in which VR is redefining our experiences across various domains. From the thrilling worlds of virtual gaming to the innovative applications in education and therapy, and the new forms of social interaction it enables, VR is opening up possibilities that were once the realm of dreams.

Join me as we delve into the world of virtual reality, uncover its history, understand its present, and envision its future. Together, we'll explore how this transformative technology is reshaping our understanding of what is possible and how we, as humans, experience the world. Welcome to the journey of redefining reality.

2

The Evolution of Entertainment

THE EVOLUTION OF ENTERTAINMENT

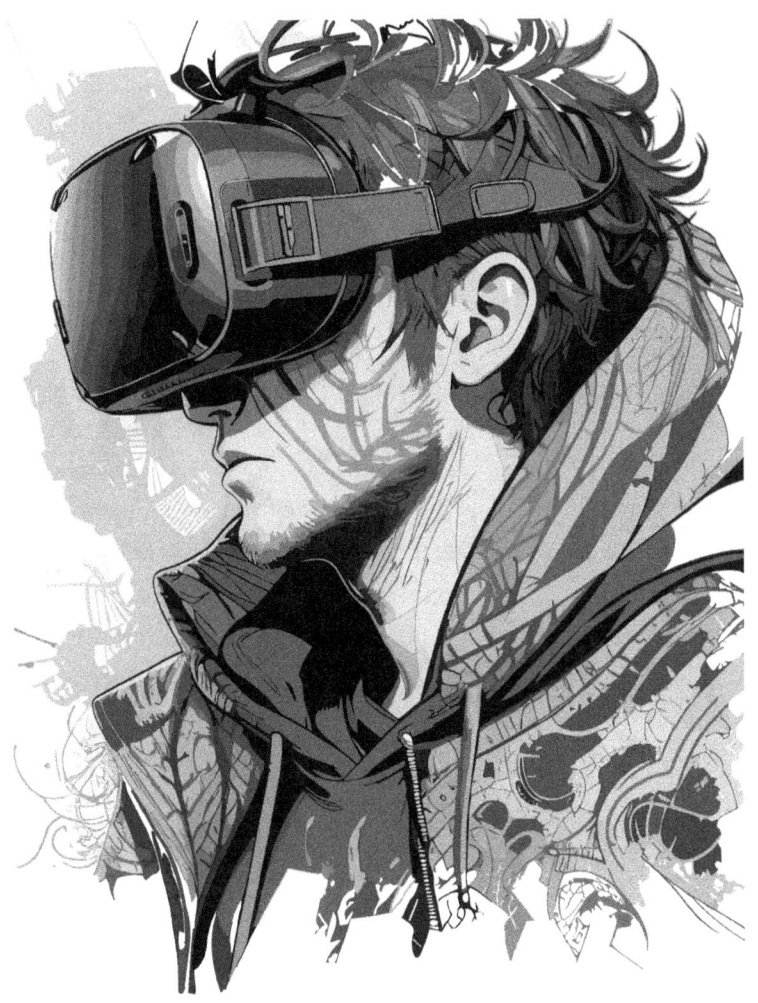

I magine strapping on a headset and instantly being transported to a different world. You find yourself in the midst of a medieval battle, defending your castle against an onslaught of invaders. Or perhaps you're soaring above a futuristic cityscape, darting between skyscrapers and engaging in high-speed aerial combat. This isn't a scene from a distant future; this is the here and now of virtual reality (VR) gaming. The rise of VR technology has heralded a revolution in the entertainment industry, transforming how we play games, watch movies, and experience stories. Alongside VR, augmented reality (AR) is also making significant strides, adding another layer to our interactive experiences. In this chapter, we'll explore how VR and AR have reshaped entertainment, focusing on the gaming revolution, the emergence of virtual cinemas, and the advent of interactive storytelling.

Gaming Revolution: Immersion Like Never Before

The gaming industry has always been at the forefront of technological innovation, constantly pushing the boundaries of what's possible. When VR entered the scene, it didn't just push those boundaries; it obliterated them. Traditional gaming, confined to a flat screen and handheld controllers, suddenly felt like a thing of the past. VR introduced a new dimension to gaming, one that envelops players in fully immersive worlds.

1. The Emergence of VR Gaming

Consider the transformation brought about by games like *Beat Saber*, where players slice through blocks in time with music, feeling every beat and pulse. Or *Half-Life: Alyx*, a VR masterpiece that places players directly in the shoes of its protagonist, allowing them to interact with the environment in ways that were previously unimaginable. These games aren't just played; they are experienced. The sense of presence, the feeling of being "inside" the game, is a game-changer in the truest sense of the word.

The hardware developments have been equally impressive. The evolution from the early days of cumbersome, expensive VR setups to sleek, affordable, and wireless headsets has made VR gaming accessible to a wider audience. Companies like Oculus, HTC, and Sony have led the charge, creating devices that deliver high-quality, immersive experiences without the need for high-end gaming PCs. This accessibility has been a key factor in VR's growing popularity.

2. Social VR Gaming: Community and Collaboration

Moreover, VR gaming has fostered a sense of community and shared experience. Multiplayer VR games allow players to meet in virtual spaces, collaborate on missions, or compete in epic battles. This social aspect of VR gaming has transformed it from a solitary activity into a shared adventure, bringing people together from all over the world in ways that traditional gaming never could.

Games like *VRChat* and *Rec Room* offer platforms where players can create avatars, socialize, and play together in a variety of virtual worlds. These environments enable people to form friendships and communities, blurring the lines between the virtual and real worlds. The ability to interact with others in a shared virtual space adds a layer of depth to gaming that was previously unattainable.

3. Augmented Reality in Gaming: Blending Real and Virtual Worlds

While VR creates entirely new worlds, augmented reality (AR) enhances the real world by overlaying digital elements onto it. AR gaming has gained significant traction with the success of games like *Pokémon GO*, which uses AR to bring Pokémon into the real world. Players use their smartphones to find and capture Pokémon in their actual surroundings, blending the digital and physical realms.

AR gaming extends beyond smartphones with devices like the Microsoft HoloLens and Magic Leap, which offer more immersive AR experiences. These headsets project holographic images into the real world, allowing players to interact with digital elements as if they were physically present. AR gaming opens up new possibilities for location-based experiences, treasure hunts, and interactive storytelling that integrate seamlessly with the real world.

Virtual Cinemas: A New Way to Experience Film

Imagine being part of your favorite movie, not just as a passive viewer but as an active participant. Virtual reality has made this possible, creating a new genre of entertainment where the lines between film and experience blur. Virtual cinemas are at the forefront of this innovation, offering audiences a way to immerse themselves in cinematic worlds like never before.

1. Immersive Film Experiences

One of the pioneers in this field is *Baobab Studios*, known for its VR short films like *Invasion!* and *Asteroids!*. These experiences place viewers at the center of the action, allowing them to interact with characters and influence the storyline. The result is a level of engagement that traditional films can't match. Instead of just watching the protagonist escape danger, viewers in a virtual cinema might find themselves helping to solve puzzles or navigate obstacles, becoming integral to the unfolding narrative.

Another notable example is *Dear Angelica*, an immersive VR film by Oculus Story Studio. The film is a dreamlike exploration of memory and grief, where viewers float through hand-drawn scenes that evolve around them. The ability to look around and choose what to focus on makes each viewing experience unique and deeply personal.

2. Social VR Viewing: Recreating the Theater Experience

Virtual cinemas also offer unique social experiences. Platforms like *Bigscreen* allow users to watch movies together in a virtual theater, complete with customizable avatars and environments. This social aspect of VR cinema brings back the communal experience of going to the movies, which has been increasingly lost in the age of streaming services. Friends can gather, discuss the film in real-time, and share the experience despite being miles apart in the real world.

The sense of presence and togetherness in these virtual theaters is enhanced by the ability to interact with fellow viewers, share reactions, and even throw virtual popcorn. This communal aspect adds a layer of fun and engagement, making the virtual movie-going experience feel more like a social event.

3. Augmented Reality in Filmmaking

While VR offers immersive environments, augmented reality provides filmmakers with tools to enhance storytelling in the real world. AR can be used to create interactive movie posters, trailers, and experiences that engage audiences in new ways. For instance, using an AR app, viewers can scan a movie poster to see characters come to life, watch exclusive clips, or access behind-the-scenes content.

AR also opens up possibilities for location-based storytelling. Imagine walking through a city and encountering AR scenes from a film that took place there. These interactive elements can provide deeper context and enrich the viewing experience by connecting the film's narrative with the physical world.

Interactive Storytelling: Shaping Your Own Narrative

Storytelling has always been a fundamental part of human culture, evolving from oral traditions to written works, and eventually to film and television. With VR and AR, storytelling has taken another leap forward, becoming a fully interactive experience where users are not just passive recipients but active participants.

1. VR Interactive Narratives

Take *Wolves in the Walls*, a VR experience based on the book by Neil Gaiman and Dave McKean. In this story, users join Lucy, a young girl who believes that wolves live within the walls of her house. As the narrative unfolds, users interact with Lucy and her environment, helping her uncover the truth. This level of interaction creates a deep sense of empathy and connection with the characters, making the story more impactful and personal.

Interactive storytelling in VR goes beyond simply choosing different paths or endings. It allows for real-time interaction with the narrative and environment. In *The Under Presents*, a VR experience by Tender Claws, users are not just spectators but also performers. They interact with live actors and other participants, creating a unique blend of theater and gaming. Each user's experience is different, shaped by their actions and decisions.

2. AR and Transmedia Storytelling

AR adds another layer to interactive storytelling by merging digital narratives with the physical world. Transmedia storytelling, which involves telling a story across multiple platforms and formats, is enhanced by AR's ability to overlay narrative elements onto real-world environments.

For example, the AR experience *The Walking Dead: Our World* turns the real world into a battleground against zombies. Players can find and interact with characters from the show, complete missions, and discover story elements in their own neighborhoods. This integration of AR into transmedia storytelling creates a more immersive and engaging experience, blurring the lines between fiction and reality.

3. Educational and Training Applications

Interactive storytelling through VR and AR is not limited to entertainment; it also has significant educational and training applications. For instance, VR can be used to create historical reenactments where students can experience events from the past and make decisions that influence the outcome. This approach fosters a deeper understanding of historical events and their complexities.

In corporate training, interactive VR scenarios can simulate real-world challenges, allowing employees to practice problem-solving and decision-making skills. AR can overlay instructional content onto physical objects, providing step-by-step guidance for complex tasks. These interactive storytelling methods enhance learning by making it more engaging and hands-on.

The Technological Backbone: Hardware and Software Innovations

The evolution of VR and AR entertainment would not be possible without the continuous advancements in hardware and software. From high-resolution displays to sophisticated motion tracking, these innovations are driving the industry forward.

1. VR Headsets and Motion Controllers

The development of VR headsets has been pivotal in creating immersive experiences. Early VR systems were bulky and expensive, but modern headsets like the Oculus Rift, HTC Vive, and PlayStation VR offer high-quality visuals and comfortable designs. These headsets feature advanced motion tracking, which allows users to move naturally within the virtual environment.

Motion controllers, such as the Oculus Touch and the Vive controllers, enhance interactivity by providing precise hand tracking. These devices enable users to manipulate objects, perform gestures, and interact with the virtual world in intuitive ways. Haptic feedback adds another layer of realism, allowing users to feel textures and resistance.

2. AR Devices and Mobile Integration

AR relies heavily on mobile devices and specialized headsets to overlay digital content onto the real world. Smartphones and tablets equipped with AR capabilities have made AR accessible to a

broad audience. Apps like Pokémon GO and Snapchat's AR filters have popularized the technology, showcasing its potential for interactive experiences.

Headsets like the Microsoft HoloLens and Magic Leap One offer more advanced AR capabilities, projecting holographic images into the user's field of view. These devices use sophisticated sensors and cameras to map the physical environment, allowing digital content to interact seamlessly with real-world objects.

3. Software Platforms and Development Tools

The software platforms and development tools used to create VR and AR experiences are continually evolving. Game engines like Unity and Unreal Engine have become essential tools for developers, providing robust frameworks for building interactive environments. These engines support VR and AR development, offering features like physics simulation, lighting, and AI.

Specialized software like Tilt Brush and Quill allow artists to create 3D content within VR, while platforms like ARKit and ARCore enable developers to build AR applications for mobile devices. These tools democratize the creation of VR and AR content, empowering a new generation of creators to explore the possibilities of immersive storytelling.

The Future of VR and AR in Entertainment

As we look to the future, the potential for VR and AR in entertainment is boundless. With continuous advancements in technology and an ever-growing library of content, these mediums are poised to become integral parts of our daily lives.

1. Expanding Content Libraries

The content available for VR and AR is expanding rapidly, with developers creating experiences across a wide range of genres and formats. From epic fantasy adventures to intimate personal stories, the diversity of content ensures that there is something for everyone. This growth in content is crucial for the mainstream adoption of VR and AR, as it provides users with a wealth of experiences to explore.

2. Enhanced Realism and Immersion

Future advancements in hardware and software will enhance the realism and immersion of VR and AR experiences. Higher resolution displays, improved motion tracking, and advanced haptic feedback will create more lifelike interactions. Eye-tracking technology, which allows for more natural and responsive interactions, is also on the horizon, promising to further blur the line between the virtual and real worlds.

3. Integration with Other Technologies

The integration of VR and AR with other emerging technologies will open up new possibilities for entertainment. For example, combining VR with artificial intelligence (AI) can create more dynamic and responsive environments, where virtual characters react intelligently to user actions. Similarly, integrating AR with the Internet of Things (IoT) can create interactive smart environments, where digital content enhances real-world objects and spaces.

4. Social and Collaborative Experiences

The social and collaborative potential of VR and AR is vast. Future platforms will likely emphasize shared experiences, allowing users to connect, collaborate, and create together in virtual and augmented spaces. These social experiences will redefine how we interact with entertainment, fostering a sense of community and connection that transcends physical boundaries.

Conclusion: Embracing the Virtual Frontier

The evolution of entertainment through virtual and augmented reality is just beginning. As technology continues to advance, the possibilities for VR and AR in gaming, filmmaking, and storytelling are boundless. What we are witnessing is not just a technological innovation but a fundamental shift in how we experience and interact with stories and worlds.

Virtual and augmented reality have the power to transport us to places we've never been, to let us live experiences we've only dreamed of, and to connect us with people in ways that transcend physical boundaries. These mediums are redefining reality, pushing the limits of our imagination, and opening up new frontiers in entertainment.

As we continue to explore this exciting new landscape, one thing is clear: VR and AR are not just changing how we play games or watch movies; they're changing how we understand and experience reality itself. And this is only the beginning. Welcome to the future of entertainment. Welcome to the world of virtual and augmented reality.

3

Educational Frontiers

VIRTUAL REALITY AND HUMAN EXPERIENCE: REDEFINING REALITY

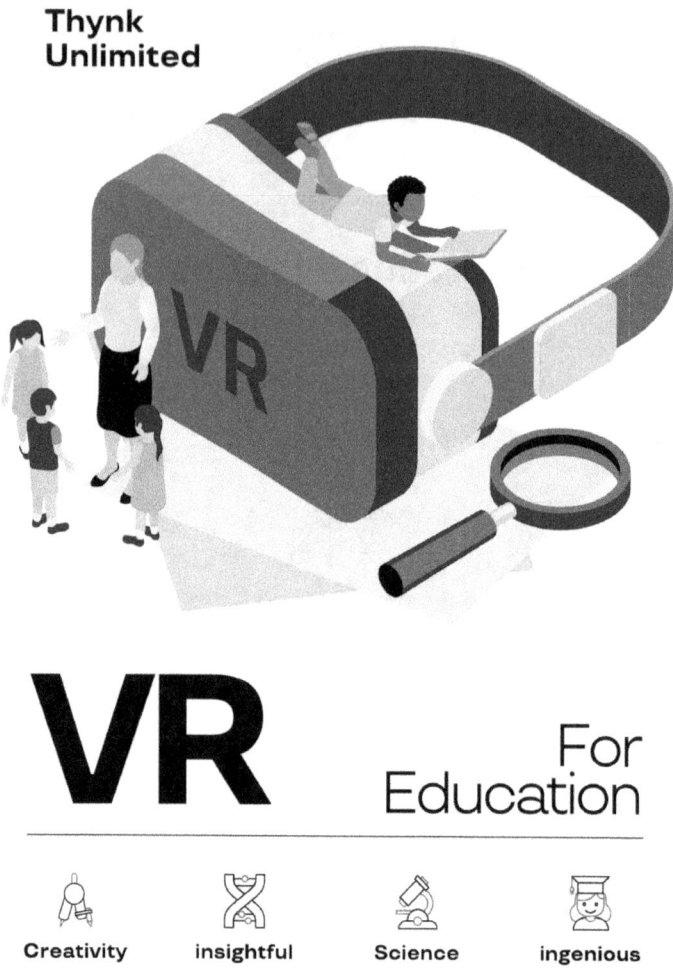

Thynk Unlimited

VR For Education

Creativity · insightful · Science · ingenious

I magine walking through the ancient streets of Rome, feeling the cobblestones beneath your feet as you pass the bustling marketplace and admire the grandeur of the Colosseum. Or perhaps you're floating inside the bloodstream, navigating through veins and arteries, observing red blood cells and platelets at work. These are not scenes from a science fiction novel but real experiences made possible by the incredible technology of virtual reality (VR). In this chapter, we will explore how VR is transforming education, creating immersive learning environments, enabling virtual classrooms, and revolutionizing professional training simulations.

Immersive Learning Environments: Breathing Life into History, Science, and Geography

Education has always been about bringing subjects to life, but VR takes this to a whole new level. Imagine studying history not just from textbooks but by walking through historical events and witnessing them firsthand. VR allows students to step back in time and experience history as if they were actually there.

1. Reimagining History Education

Take, for example, the VR application *TimeLooper*, which transports users to pivotal moments in history. Students can witness the signing of the Declaration of Independence, stand on the battlefield of Gettysburg, or even walk the streets of 16th-century London. This immersive approach not only makes history more engaging but also helps students develop a deeper understanding and empathy for the people and events of the past.

By wearing a VR headset, students can find themselves in the heart of the action. Imagine being in ancient Egypt, observing the construction of the pyramids, or standing beside Martin Luther King Jr. during his famous "I Have a Dream" speech. These experiences create a visceral connection to history, making the past come alive in ways that traditional textbooks and lectures cannot.

2. Transforming Science Education

Science education also benefits immensely from VR. Subjects that were once confined to diagrams and models can now be explored in three dimensions. *The Body VR* allows students to journey through the human body, observing the intricate details of organs, cells, and biological processes. This firsthand exploration makes complex scientific concepts more tangible and easier to grasp.

Consider a biology class where students can explore the anatomy of a frog without ever picking up a scalpel. Using VR, they can examine the frog's organs, understand their functions, and even see how they interact within the body. This interactive approach not only enhances understanding but also makes learning more engaging and fun.

Physics, too, takes on a new dimension with VR. Concepts like gravity, electromagnetism, and quantum mechanics can be visualized in 3D environments, helping students to better understand abstract ideas. For instance, VR simulations can demonstrate the behavior of particles in a collider or the effects of gravitational waves, making complex theories more accessible.

3. Revolutionizing Geography Education

Geography, too, is being transformed by VR. Platforms like *Google Earth VR* enable students to explore the farthest corners of the globe without leaving their classrooms. They can traverse the Amazon rainforest, climb Mount Everest, or dive into the Great Barrier Reef. This virtual exploration fosters a sense of curiosity and adventure, encouraging students to learn about different cultures and ecosystems in a more interactive and meaningful way.

Imagine a geography lesson where students can explore the impact of climate change on Arctic ice caps, witness deforestation in the Amazon, or tour the world's most significant natural landmarks. VR allows students to experience these phenomena firsthand, deepening their understanding and fostering a sense of global citizenship.

In addition to natural landscapes, VR can also bring cultural and urban environments to life. Students can take virtual field trips to cities like Tokyo, Paris, or New York, exploring their landmarks, museums, and neighborhoods. This immersive approach helps students appreciate the diversity and complexity of our world, enhancing their cultural awareness and empathy.

Virtual Classrooms: Breaking Down Barriers

One of the most significant impacts of VR in education is its ability to break down geographical barriers and make learning accessible to everyone, regardless of location. Virtual classrooms are becoming a game-changer, especially for remote and underserved areas.

1. Creating Global Classrooms

Imagine a student in a rural village attending a virtual classroom with peers from around the world. In *AltspaceVR*, an application that creates virtual social spaces, students can gather in a virtual classroom, interact with their teacher and classmates, and participate in discussions as if they were in a physical room. This sense of presence and community, despite physical distances, is one of VR's most powerful features.

In these virtual classrooms, students can engage in real-time discussions, collaborate on projects, and participate in interactive lessons. The immersive nature of VR makes these experiences feel more authentic and engaging than traditional online learning platforms. By breaking down geographical barriers, VR classrooms foster a sense of global community and collaboration, preparing students for an increasingly interconnected world.

2. Enhancing Accessibility and Inclusivity

Virtual classrooms also offer unique opportunities for specialized education. For instance, *ENGAGE VR* is a platform designed specifically for educational purposes, providing virtual spaces for lectures, workshops, and collaborative projects. Teachers can create interactive lessons with 3D models and simulations, making abstract concepts more concrete. Students can manipulate molecules in chemistry, explore the architecture of ancient civilizations, or even perform virtual dissections in biology class.

Moreover, VR can accommodate diverse learning styles and needs. For students with disabilities, VR can offer customized environments that cater to their specific requirements, making education more inclusive. For example, students with mobility impairments can explore virtual environments without physical limitations, and those with autism can practice social interactions in controlled, virtual settings.

Consider a student with a hearing impairment attending a VR classroom where sign language interpreters and real-time captions are integrated seamlessly into the environment. Or think of a student with ADHD who benefits from the immersive and interactive nature of VR, which helps maintain their focus and engagement. VR's flexibility and adaptability make it a powerful tool for creating inclusive educational experiences that cater to the needs of all learners.

3. Facilitating Lifelong Learning

The rise of virtual classrooms also supports lifelong learning, providing opportunities for continuing education and professional development. Adults can attend virtual workshops, seminars, and training sessions, gaining new skills and knowledge without the constraints of location or time. This flexibility is particularly valuable for working professionals, parents, and others with busy schedules.

For instance, a nurse in a remote area can attend a virtual seminar on the latest medical advancements, or a software developer can participate in a VR coding bootcamp to learn a new programming language. These opportunities for lifelong learning help individuals stay current in their fields, advance their careers, and adapt to the changing demands of the workforce.

Training Simulations: Preparing for the Real World

Professional training is another area where VR is making a significant impact. In fields where hands-on experience is crucial, VR provides a safe and effective way to practice and hone skills.

1. Medical Training: Precision and Practice

In medicine, for example, VR training simulations are revolutionizing how surgeons prepare for complex procedures. *Osso VR* offers realistic surgical simulations that allow medical students and professionals to practice surgeries repeatedly until they achieve proficiency. These simulations provide detailed feedback, helping trainees improve their techniques and reduce the risk of errors in real-life surgeries. This not only enhances the learning experience but also significantly improves patient safety.

Imagine a medical student practicing a delicate surgery on a virtual patient, receiving real-time feedback on their technique and precision. By practicing in a virtual environment, they can build confidence and competence before ever stepping into an operating room. This approach not only enhances surgical skills but also reduces the stress and anxiety associated with high-stakes procedures.

2. Engineering and Technical Training: Building Skills and Confidence

Engineering is another field benefiting from VR training simulations. Engineers can use VR to design and test structures in a virtual environment before building them in the real world. This allows for more innovative designs and helps identify potential issues early in the process. For instance, automotive engineers at companies like Ford are using VR to create and test car prototypes, making the design process more efficient and cost-effective.

In addition to design and testing, VR can also be used for training in technical skills. For example, an aspiring electrician can practice wiring a virtual house, learning the intricacies of electrical systems without the risk of injury. Similarly, a construction worker can practice operating heavy machinery in a virtual environment, building their skills and confidence before working on a real construction site.

3. Aviation Training: Safety and Precision

Aviation training has also been transformed by VR. Pilots can now undergo extensive training in virtual flight simulators that replicate real-world flying conditions. These simulators, such as those developed by *FlyInside*, provide a realistic and immersive experience, allowing pilots to practice emergency procedures and flight maneuvers in a safe environment. This type of training is invaluable, as it helps pilots build confidence and competence without the risks associated with real-world practice.

Consider a pilot practicing an emergency landing in a VR simulator, experiencing the challenges and pressures of the situation without the real-world consequences. By repeatedly practicing these scenarios, pilots can build the skills and confidence needed to handle emergencies effectively. This approach not only enhances pilot training but also improves overall aviation safety.

4. Law Enforcement and Military Training: Realism and Preparedness

Law enforcement and military training are other areas where VR is making a significant impact. VR simulations can create realistic scenarios for training purposes, allowing officers and soldiers to practice their skills in a controlled and immersive environment. Whether it's a hostage situation, a firefight, or a disaster response, VR training helps prepare individuals for the challenges they may face in the field.

For example, a police officer can practice de-escalation techniques in a virtual scenario, learning to handle high-stress situations with calm and precision. Similarly, soldiers can train for combat missions in realistic VR environments, improving their tactical skills and decision-making abilities. These immersive simulations help build the readiness and resilience needed for real-world operations.

Conclusion: The Dawn of a New Educational Era

The integration of VR into education marks the beginning of a new era, one where learning
   is not confined by the limitations of physical space and traditional

methods. VR has the power to make education more engaging, accessible, and effective, opening up a world of possibilities for students and professionals alike.

As we continue to explore and develop this technology, the potential for VR in education will only grow. Imagine a future where students from all corners of the globe can learn together in virtual classrooms, where complex scientific concepts can be understood through immersive simulations, and where professionals can perfect their skills through realistic training environments.

The educational frontiers of VR are vast and exciting, promising to transform how we teach, learn, and grow. As we venture further into this brave new world, we carry with us the hope that VR will not only enhance our understanding of the world but also inspire a lifelong love of learning. Welcome to the future of education, where reality is just the beginning.

4

Therapeutic Applications

THERAPEUTIC APPLICATIONS

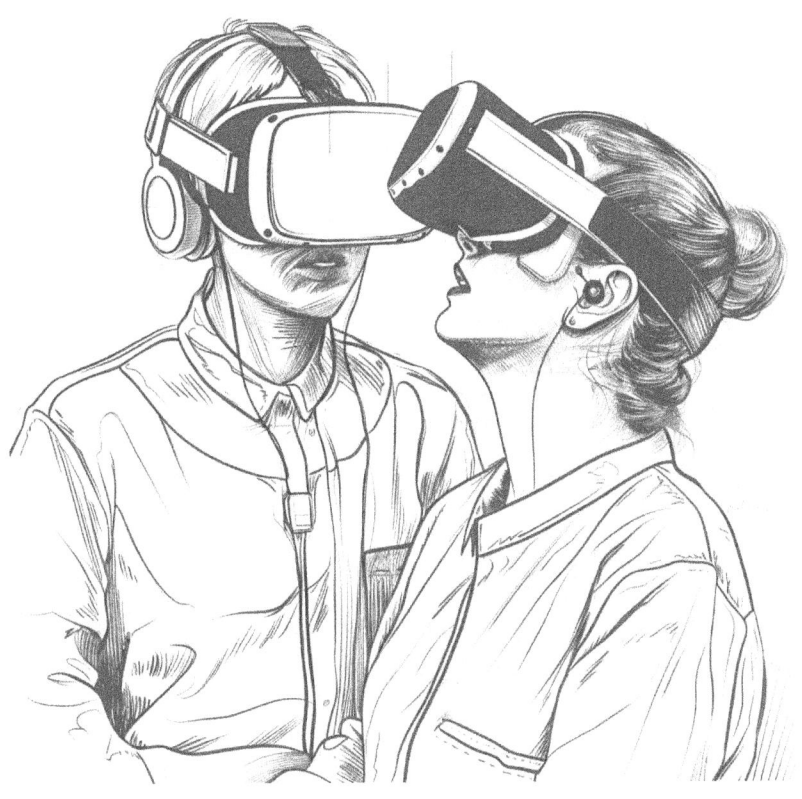

I n the quiet chambers of the mind, battles are fought and scars are born. For those grappling with mental health disorders like post-traumatic stress disorder (PTSD), anxiety, and phobias, the journey to healing can be long and arduous. Enter virtual reality (VR), a realm where healing begins with a single step into the unknown. As we delve into the therapeutic applications of VR, we uncover a world where technology meets compassion, transforming the landscape of mental health, physical rehabilitation, and cognitive therapy.

Mental Health: Healing the Invisible Wounds

Mental health has long been a realm where traditional therapies struggle to reach, with invisible wounds often left unattended. However, the emergence of VR therapy offers a new avenue for healing, one that harnesses the power of immersive technology to confront trauma and reclaim control.

1. PTSD Treatment: Rewriting the Past

For veterans haunted by the ghosts of war, VR therapy offers a path to peace. Through immersive simulations, individuals can confront their traumatic memories in a safe and controlled environment, gradually desensitizing themselves to triggers and reclaiming their sense of control. Organizations like Bravemind use VR to recreate combat scenarios, allowing veterans to revisit their experiences and process their emotions in a therapeutic setting. The success of VR in treating PTSD lies in its ability to immerse patients in a virtual world that feels real, yet is controlled and safe.

2. Anxiety and Phobia Treatment: Confronting Fears

Anxiety disorders, too, are met with courage and resilience in the virtual realm. Whether it's fear of heights, flying, or social situations, VR exposure therapy provides a lifeline to those struggling to overcome their fears. Through immersive simulations, individuals can confront their anxieties head-on, gradually building confidence and mastery until fear gives way to freedom. This approach not only reduces anxiety symptoms but also equips patients with valuable coping skills they can carry into their daily lives.

In a typical VR therapy session for anxiety, a patient might begin by experiencing a mild version of their feared situation. For instance, someone with a fear of flying might start by sitting in a virtual airplane on the tarmac. Over time, the scenarios can become more intense, with the patient experiencing takeoff, turbulence, and landing. Each step is carefully monitored by a therapist, who can adjust the difficulty and provide support as needed.

3. Innovative Uses of VR in Mental Health

The applications of VR in mental health extend beyond traditional exposure therapy. Innovative uses include VR-based mindfulness and relaxation programs, which immerse users in tranquil environments such as beaches or forests, helping them practice relaxation techniques and reduce stress. Additionally, VR is being used to simulate social interactions, providing a safe space for individuals with social anxiety to practice and improve their social skills.

Physical Rehabilitation: A Journey of Movement and Strength

In the realm of physical rehabilitation, where every step is a victory and every movement a triumph, VR emerges as a powerful ally in the quest for healing. For those recovering from injuries, surgeries, or chronic conditions, VR therapy offers a pathway to recovery that is as engaging as it is effective.

1. Interactive Exercise Programs

Imagine a world where rehabilitation is not confined to sterile hospital rooms but unfolds in vibrant, immersive landscapes where every movement is a step toward healing. In VR physical therapy, patients can engage in interactive exercises that target specific muscle groups, improve range of motion, and enhance balance and coordination. Whether it's walking along a virtual beach or climbing a virtual mountain, patients are empowered to take charge of their recovery in a way that feels both natural and empowering.

These interactive exercises can be tailored to the individual needs of each patient. For example, a person recovering from knee surgery might use a VR program that guides them through gentle stretches and strengthening exercises. The immersive nature of VR makes the exercises more engaging, reducing the monotony that often accompanies traditional physical therapy.

2. Realistic Scenario-Based Training

But VR therapy isn't just about physical movement; it's also about the power of the mind to heal the body. By immersing patients in realistic scenarios that mimic everyday activities, VR therapy helps bridge the gap between rehabilitation and real life, enabling patients to practice essential skills in a safe and supportive environment. For stroke survivors, for example, VR simulations can facilitate hand-eye coordination exercises, improve fine motor skills, and enhance overall functional independence.

One such application is a VR program that simulates activities of daily living. Patients can practice tasks like grocery shopping, cooking, or navigating their homes. These simulations help patients regain confidence in their abilities and prepare them for the challenges they will face when they return to their daily lives.

3. Enhancing Motivation and Adherence

A critical factor in the success of any rehabilitation program is patient adherence. Traditional physical therapy can be repetitive and boring, leading to low motivation and poor compliance. VR therapy addresses this issue by making rehabilitation exercises more engaging and enjoyable. Gamified elements, such as earning points for completing tasks or competing against oneself in a virtual environment, can significantly enhance motivation and adherence.

Cognitive Therapy: Navigating the Labyrinth of the Mind

In the labyrinth of the mind, where thoughts twist and turn like winding pathways, VR therapy offers a guiding light, illuminating the way forward for those grappling with cognitive challenges. Whether it's memory loss, attention deficits, or executive function impairments, VR therapy provides a beacon of hope for individuals seeking to reclaim their cognitive abilities and restore their sense of self.

1. Cognitive Stimulation for Neurological Conditions

For those living with neurological conditions like Alzheimer's disease or traumatic brain injury (TBI), VR therapy offers a lifeline, providing cognitive stimulation and engagement in a way that is both enjoyable and effective. By immersing patients in interactive environments that challenge their cognitive abilities, VR therapy helps to preserve memory, improve attention and concentration, and enhance overall cognitive function. Activities like virtual puzzles, memory games, and cognitive exercises offer a holistic approach to rehabilitation, targeting multiple areas of cognitive functioning simultaneously.

In one such program, patients with Alzheimer's can explore a virtual garden where they can engage in activities designed to stimulate memory and cognitive skills. For example, they might be tasked with remembering the locations of different flowers or completing a series of steps to care for a virtual plant. These activities not only provide cognitive stimulation but also offer a sense of accomplishment and enjoyment.

THERAPEUTIC APPLICATIONS

2. Neurorehabilitation: Promoting Neuroplasticity

Moreover, VR therapy holds promise as a tool for neurorehabilitation, aiding in the recovery of brain function following injury or illness. By stimulating neural pathways and promoting neuroplasticity, VR therapy helps to restore lost function and facilitate recovery in individuals with neurological deficits. Whether it's regaining language skills, improving motor function, or enhancing spatial awareness, VR therapy offers a dynamic and immersive approach to neurorehabilitation that is as effective as it is engaging.

For instance, VR programs designed for stroke rehabilitation might include tasks that require patients to reach for and manipulate virtual objects, helping to rebuild motor skills and coordination. These programs can be customized to the patient's level of ability, providing a gradual progression of difficulty that supports continuous improvement.

3. Addressing Cognitive Behavioral Therapy (CBT)

Cognitive Behavioral Therapy (CBT) is a widely used approach for treating a variety of mental health conditions, including depression, anxiety, and PTSD. VR can enhance CBT by providing immersive environments where patients can practice new skills and behaviors. For example, a VR program might simulate social interactions, allowing patients to practice assertiveness, communication skills, and coping strategies in a safe and controlled setting.

In a VR-based CBT program for social anxiety, patients might participate in virtual social gatherings, practice initiating conversations, and learn to manage anxiety-provoking situations. The immersive nature of VR makes these exercises more realistic and effective, helping patients to build confidence and apply their skills in real-life situations.

Case Studies and Real-World Applications

To understand the impact of VR therapy, let's delve into some real-world examples and case studies that highlight its transformative potential.

1. Bravemind and PTSD

Bravemind, developed by the University of Southern California Institute for Creative Technologies, is a VR-based therapy program designed to treat PTSD. The program recreates combat scenarios based on the patient's traumatic experiences. During therapy sessions, patients wear a VR headset and navigate through these virtual environments, guided by a therapist.

One veteran who used Bravemind described the experience as challenging but ultimately healing. By repeatedly confronting and processing his traumatic memories in a controlled environment, he was able to reduce his PTSD symptoms and regain a sense of normalcy in his life. This case highlights the power of VR to provide immersive, effective therapy for individuals struggling with PTSD.

2. VR in Stroke Rehabilitation

In stroke rehabilitation, VR programs like the ones developed by MindMaze are making significant strides. MindMaze's MindMotion PRO is a VR-based neurorehabilitation platform that provides engaging and interactive therapy for stroke survivors. The platform includes a range of activities designed to improve motor function, coordination, and cognitive skills.

A stroke survivor who used MindMotion PRO shared her story of recovery, describing how the VR exercises helped her regain strength and coordination in her affected limbs. The immersive nature of the therapy made the exercises enjoyable, motivating her to stick with the program and achieve significant improvements in her functional abilities.

3. VR for Autism Spectrum Disorder (ASD)

For individuals with Autism Spectrum Disorder (ASD), VR offers a unique tool for social skills training. Programs like Floreo use VR to create safe and controlled environments where individuals with ASD can practice social interactions and build essential communication skills.

One case study involved a young boy with ASD who used Floreo's VR program to practice making eye contact, understanding social cues, and engaging in conversations. Over time, his social skills improved, and he became more confident in social situations. This example demonstrates how VR can provide targeted and effective interventions for individuals with ASD, helping them navigate social interactions and build meaningful connections.

Conclusion: A Journey of Healing and Hope

In the tapestry of life, where threads of pain and suffering are woven with threads of resilience and hope, virtual reality emerges as a transformative force for healing. From the depths of mental anguish to the challenges of physical rehabilitation and the complexities of cognitive therapy, VR therapy offers a beacon of light in the darkness, guiding individuals on a journey of healing and self-discovery.

As we continue to unlock the potential of VR therapy, the possibilities for healing are as boundless as the imagination itself. Whether it's confronting traumatic memories, reclaiming physical strength, or restoring cognitive function, VR therapy offers a pathway to healing that is as unique as the individuals it serves. In the end, it is not just about overcoming obstacles or achieving milestones; it's about reclaiming what was lost and embracing the journey of healing and hope that lies ahead.

Welcome to the world of virtual reality therapy, where healing begins with a single step into the unknown. With each advance in technology, we move closer to a future where VR is an integral part of therapeutic practice, offering new possibilities for healing and growth. As we venture further into this brave new world, we carry with us the hope that VR will not only enhance our understanding of the mind and body but also inspire a new era of compassionate and effective therapy.

The journey is just beginning, and the potential for transformation is immense. Together, we can explore the therapeutic frontiers of VR, harnessing its power to heal and transform lives. Welcome to the future of therapy, where reality is redefined, and healing knows no bounds.

5

Social Interaction and Virtual Communities

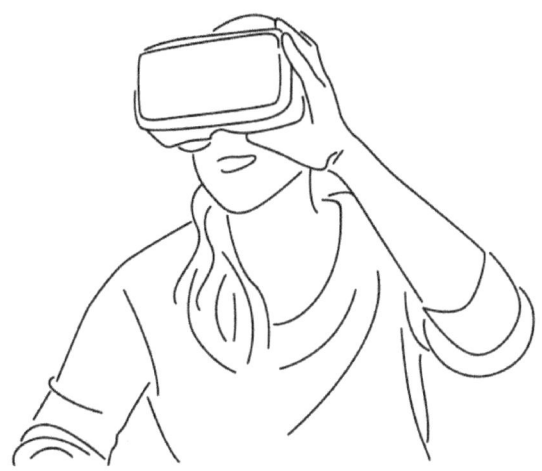

I magine entering a bustling digital marketplace, avatars of people from around the globe milling about, engaging in conversations, sharing experiences, and even forming lasting relationships. In this vibrant virtual world, the limitations of physical distance vanish, and the possibilities for social interaction expand infinitely. This is the promise of virtual reality (VR) and augmented reality (AR), technologies that are reshaping how we connect, communicate, and form communities. In this chapter, we'll delve into the transformative power of VR and AR in social interaction and virtual communities, exploring virtual social spaces, virtual events and gatherings, and the impact on relationships.

Virtual Social Spaces: Building Digital Worlds Together

In the beginning, the internet was a vast and lonely place. Email and chatrooms allowed for communication, but they lacked the depth and richness of face-to-face interactions. Then came social media, bridging the gap and bringing people closer. Now, VR and AR are taking the next leap, creating immersive social spaces where users can interact in ways that feel almost as real as being there in person.

1. Virtual Reality Social Platforms

Platforms like *VRChat*, *AltspaceVR*, and *Rec Room* are at the forefront of this revolution. In *VRChat*, users create customized avatars and explore a myriad of user-generated worlds, from fantastical landscapes to realistic recreations of famous cities. Here, social interactions are not limited to text or voice; they encompass body language, gestures, and spatial audio, creating a more natural and engaging experience.

Imagine attending a virtual party in a stunningly recreated Paris, chatting with friends while the Eiffel Tower twinkles in the background. In these spaces, users can play games, attend events, and even create their own virtual environments. The ability to customize and inhabit these worlds fosters a deep sense of ownership and community.

2. Augmented Reality Social Interactions

While VR creates entirely new worlds, AR enhances our existing reality. Applications like *Pokémon GO* and *Harry Potter: Wizards Unite* have shown how AR can bring people together in the real world. These games encourage players to explore their surroundings, interact with digital elements, and collaborate with others in real-world locations.

AR social platforms, such as *Spatial*, allow users to overlay digital content onto their physical environment, facilitating remote collaboration and social interaction. Imagine holding a virtual meeting where participants appear as holograms in your living room, or attending a virtual art show where the exhibits are projected onto the walls of a gallery. AR enhances social interactions by adding a layer of digital richness to our everyday experiences.

3. Creating Inclusive and Diverse Communities

One of the most profound impacts of VR and AR social spaces is their potential to create inclusive and diverse communities. In these digital worlds, physical disabilities, geographic barriers, and social stigmas dissolve. People can interact as equals, represented by avatars that reflect their true selves or the selves they wish to be.

For instance, in VRChat, users have the freedom to choose avatars that may not correspond to their physical appearance, allowing them to explore different aspects of their identity in a supportive and accepting environment. This freedom fosters a sense of belonging and empowerment, helping individuals form connections that might be difficult to establish in the physical world.

Virtual Events and Gatherings: Redefining Social Experiences

The COVID-19 pandemic underscored the importance of staying connected even when physically apart. Virtual events and gatherings emerged as essential tools for maintaining social bonds. With VR and AR, these events are no longer limited to flat screens and video calls; they become immersive experiences that engage all the senses.

1. Virtual Concerts and Performances

Imagine attending a concert where you can stand right next to the stage, feeling the thump of the bass and the energy of the crowd, all from the comfort of your living room. Platforms like *Wave* and *NextVR* have pioneered virtual concerts, where artists perform in digital venues, and fans can interact with each other and the performers.

In a *Wave* concert, for example, fans can dance, cheer, and even send virtual gifts to the performers. These experiences replicate the excitement and communal atmosphere of live concerts, offering a sense of presence and connection that transcends physical boundaries.

2. Virtual Conferences and Meetings

Business and academic conferences have also embraced VR and AR. Platforms like *VirBELA* and *Engage* provide virtual environments for professional gatherings, complete with auditoriums, breakout rooms, and networking spaces. Participants can attend keynotes, engage in panel discussions, and collaborate on projects, all within a virtual space that feels more interactive and engaging than traditional video calls.

These virtual conferences offer unique advantages, such as the ability to create detailed simulations and interactive presentations. For example, an engineering firm might use a VR conference to demonstrate a new product, allowing attendees to interact with a 3D model and explore its features in detail.

3. Virtual Festivals and Gatherings

Cultural events and festivals have also found a home in virtual spaces. *The Burning Man* festival, traditionally held in the Nevada desert, created a virtual version called *Burning Man Multiverse*, allowing participants to explore virtual camps, attend workshops, and connect with fellow burners from around the world.

These virtual gatherings preserve the spirit and community of physical events while expanding their reach. Participants can join from anywhere in the world, bringing diverse perspectives and experiences to the event. The virtual format also allows for creative experimentation, with artists and organizers pushing the boundaries of what's possible in a digital space.

Impact on Relationships: Connecting Hearts Across Distances

The ability of VR and AR to create immersive and engaging social experiences has profound implications for personal relationships. From friendships to romantic connections, these technologies are reshaping how we form and maintain bonds.

1. Long-Distance Relationships

For couples separated by distance, VR offers a way to bridge the gap. Virtual environments allow partners to spend time together in a shared space, whether it's a cozy virtual home, a scenic beach, or a bustling city. In these spaces, they can engage in activities, watch movies, and even cook virtual meals together, creating a sense of presence and intimacy.

Imagine a couple in a long-distance relationship meeting in a virtual café for a date night, complete with ambient sounds, virtual food, and the ability to see each other's avatars. This level of immersion helps maintain emotional connections and can alleviate the loneliness and isolation that often accompany long-distance relationships.

2. Friendships and Social Circles

VR and AR also offer new ways to maintain and strengthen friendships. Friends can meet in virtual spaces to play games, explore new worlds, or simply hang out and chat. These interactions feel more personal and engaging than traditional online communication, fostering deeper connections.

For instance, a group of friends might meet in a VR game like *Rec Room* to complete challenges together, or they might gather in *AltspaceVR* for a movie night. The shared experiences and the ability to interact in a more natural way help maintain the bonds of friendship, even when physical meetups are not possible.

3. Building New Relationships

The social nature of VR and AR platforms also makes them ideal for meeting new people and forming new relationships. Users can join communities and events based on their interests, making it easier to find like-minded individuals. These interactions often lead to meaningful connections and friendships.

Consider a user who loves art and joins a virtual art gallery in *Spatial*. They might meet other art enthusiasts, discuss their favorite pieces, and even collaborate on virtual art projects. These shared interests and experiences create a strong foundation for building new relationships.

Challenges and Considerations: Navigating the Virtual Social Landscape

While the potential of VR and AR in social interaction is immense, it also comes with challenges and considerations. As we navigate this new landscape, it's essential to address issues related to privacy, security, and mental health.

1. Privacy and Data Security

In virtual environments, users share a significant amount of personal information, from their avatars and interactions to biometric data collected by VR and AR devices. Ensuring the privacy and security of this data is paramount. Developers and platform providers must implement robust security measures and transparent privacy policies to protect users.

Users should also be aware of the data they share and take steps to safeguard their privacy. This includes using strong passwords, being cautious about sharing personal information, and understanding the privacy settings of the platforms they use.

2. Digital Etiquette and Harassment

As with any social platform, VR and AR environments are not immune to issues of harassment and inappropriate behavior. Establishing guidelines for digital etiquette and implementing measures to prevent and address harassment is crucial for creating safe and welcoming spaces.

Platforms can provide tools for users to report and block harassers, and moderators can help maintain a positive and respectful environment. Educating users about digital etiquette and encouraging a culture of respect and inclusion are also essential steps in fostering healthy virtual communities.

3. Mental Health and Well-Being

Spending extended periods in virtual environments can have implications for mental health and well-being. While VR and AR can enhance social connections and provide engaging experiences, it's important to maintain a balance with real-world interactions and activities.

Users should be mindful of their screen time and take breaks to engage in physical activities and face-to-face interactions. Developers can support this by creating features that encourage healthy usage patterns, such as reminders to take breaks and options to limit session durations.

The Future of Social Interaction in VR and AR

As VR and AR technologies continue to evolve, the possibilities for social interaction and virtual communities will expand even further. Here are some trends and developments to watch for in the coming years.

1. Enhanced Realism and Presence

Advancements in hardware and software will enhance the realism and presence of VR and AR experiences. Higher resolution displays, improved motion tracking, and advanced haptic feedback will create more lifelike interactions. Eye-tracking technology and facial recognition will enable avatars to reflect users' expressions and emotions more accurately, enhancing the sense of presence and connection.

2. Integration with AI and Machine Learning

The integration of AI and machine learning with VR and AR will enable more dynamic and responsive environments. Virtual characters and assistants will become more intelligent and interactive, providing personalized experiences and support. AI-driven content generation will allow for more diverse and engaging virtual worlds.

3. Expansion of Social and Collaborative Platforms

The growth of social and collaborative platforms will continue, with new applications and features that cater to a wide range of interests and needs. From professional networking and collaboration to creative expression and entertainment, these platforms will offer increasingly sophisticated tools for interaction and collaboration.

4. Cross-Platform and Cross-Reality Experiences

Future developments will likely focus on creating seamless cross-platform and cross-reality experiences. Users will be able to move fluidly between VR, AR, and traditional digital environments, carrying their identities and social connections with them. This integration will create a more cohesive and interconnected digital ecosystem.

5. Focus on Inclusivity and Accessibility

Ensuring that VR and AR experiences are inclusive and accessible to all users will remain a priority. Developers will continue to innovate in creating environments that accommodate diverse needs and preferences, making these technologies more accessible to individuals with disabilities and those in underserved communities.

Conclusion: Embracing the Virtual Community

The transformative power of VR and AR in social interaction and virtual communities is just beginning to unfold. These technologies have the potential to bring people closer together, transcending physical boundaries and creating new opportunities for connection and collaboration. As we embrace this virtual frontier, we have the chance to build inclusive, diverse, and vibrant communities that reflect the best of our shared humanity.

In this new era of social interaction, the lines between the virtual and real worlds blur, and the possibilities for connection and creativity are boundless. Whether it's meeting friends in a virtual café, attending a concert from the comfort of home, or collaborating on a project with colleagues across the globe, VR and AR offer new ways to enrich our lives and strengthen our relationships.

Welcome to the future of social interaction. Welcome to the world of virtual and augmented reality, where the only limit is our imagination.

6

Redefining Reality

VIRTUAL REALITY AND HUMAN EXPERIENCE: REDEFINING REALITY

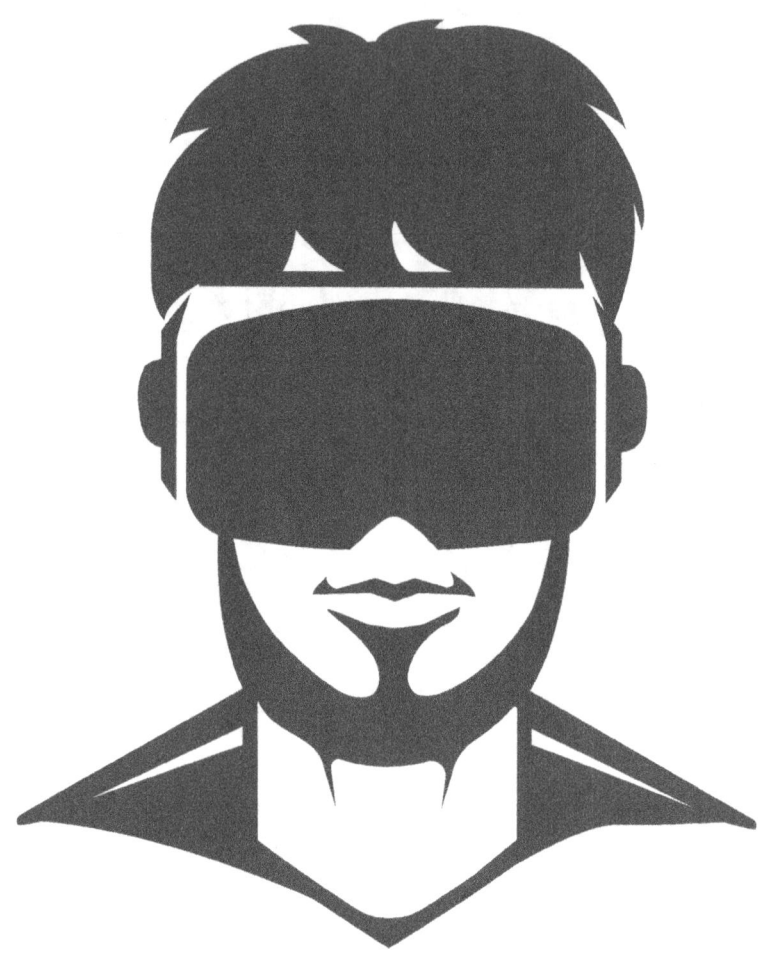

Picture a world where the boundaries between the physical and digital realms are so blurred that you can hardly distinguish one from the other. A place where you can slip between realities with a mere thought, exploring vast landscapes or intimate settings, all crafted with such precision and detail that they feel more real than reality itself. This is the frontier we are approaching with virtual reality (VR) and augmented reality (AR). In this chapter, we will explore how these technologies are redefining our perception of reality, examining perception and presence, blurring boundaries, and the profound impact on identity and self-representation.

Perception and Presence: The Psychology of Immersion

The essence of VR and AR lies in their ability to create a sense of presence, making users feel as if they are truly part of the digital environment. This immersive quality is not just a technical feat; it's a profound psychological experience that alters our perception of reality.

1. The Science of Presence

Presence, in the context of VR and AR, refers to the sensation of being physically present in a non-physical world. It's the magic that makes virtual experiences feel real. This phenomenon is rooted in the brain's ability to construct a sense of place from sensory inputs. When VR and AR systems provide consistent and coherent sensory information, our brains accept the virtual environment as reality.

Studies have shown that presence is influenced by several factors, including the quality of the graphics, the responsiveness of the system, and the level of interactivity. High-resolution visuals, realistic soundscapes, and natural user interfaces all contribute to a heightened sense of presence. But it's more than just technical specs; it's about creating a seamless experience where the user's actions have meaningful consequences in the virtual world.

2. The Impact on Perception

When we are immersed in a virtual environment, our perception of time, space, and even our own bodies can change. This phenomenon, known as "temporal dilation," can make time feel like it's passing faster or slower than it actually is. Users often report losing track of time while engaged in VR experiences, a testament to the technology's ability to fully capture our attention.

Spatial perception is also transformed. In VR, distances can feel more tangible, and objects can have a sense of weight and texture. These changes in perception are not just illusions; they are the brain's adaptive response to new sensory information. The implications are vast, influencing everything from entertainment to therapeutic applications, where manipulating perception can aid in pain management or physical rehabilitation.

Blurring Boundaries: The Convergence of Real and Virtual Worlds

As VR and AR technologies advance, the distinction between the real and virtual worlds becomes increasingly blurred. This convergence is creating new possibilities for how we interact with and understand our environment.

1. Augmented Reality: Enhancing the Real World

AR overlays digital information onto the physical world, enhancing our perception and interaction with our surroundings. Applications like *Google Lens* allow users to point their smartphones at objects to receive instant information, while AR navigation apps overlay directions onto the real world, making it easier to find our way.

Consider the use of AR in education. A biology student wearing AR glasses can see a 3D model of the human heart hovering over their textbook, with interactive labels and animations showing how blood flows through the chambers. This blend of digital and physical information makes learning more engaging and intuitive, transforming abstract concepts into tangible experiences.

2. Virtual Reality: Creating Entirely New Worlds

While AR enhances our reality, VR creates entirely new ones. These virtual worlds are limited only by imagination, offering experiences that can range from the hyper-realistic to the fantastically surreal. In VR, users can explore ancient civilizations, dive into the depths of the ocean, or soar through space, all from the comfort of their homes.

The creation of these worlds involves a combination of art and technology. Designers use advanced modeling software to build intricate environments, while developers program interactions that make these worlds feel alive. The result is a level of immersion that can transport users to places they've never been, providing a sense of adventure and exploration.

3. Mixed Reality: The Best of Both Worlds

Mixed reality (MR) combines elements of both VR and AR, allowing digital and physical objects to coexist and interact in real-time. MR systems, like the Microsoft HoloLens, use advanced sensors and AI to understand and map the physical environment, overlaying interactive holograms that respond to the user's actions.

Imagine a virtual assistant that appears in your living room to help you plan your day, or a virtual pet that interacts with real objects in your home. MR offers a seamless blend of real and virtual, opening up new possibilities for entertainment, productivity, and social interaction.

Identity and Self-Representation: The Digital Self

One of the most intriguing aspects of VR and AR is their impact on identity and self-representation. These technologies allow users to create and inhabit digital avatars, offering new ways to express themselves and interact with others.

1. Avatars and Identity Exploration

In virtual environments, users can create avatars that represent their digital selves. These avatars can be anything from realistic replicas to fantastical creatures, providing a canvas for self-expression. This freedom allows users to explore different aspects of their identity, trying on different appearances and personalities in a safe and supportive environment.

For many, this ability to experiment with identity is liberating. It can help individuals explore their gender identity, express parts of themselves that they may hide in the real world, or simply have fun with creative self-expression. The anonymity of digital avatars can also reduce social anxiety, making it easier for people to interact and form connections.

2. The Social Dynamics of Virtual Worlds

The way we interact with others in virtual environments is influenced by our avatars. Studies have shown that users often behave in ways consistent with their avatar's appearance, a phenomenon known as the "Proteus effect." For example, users with taller, more attractive avatars may exhibit more confident behavior, while those with less appealing avatars may be more reserved.

These dynamics have significant implications for social interactions in VR and AR. They can influence how we form relationships, how we perceive others, and how we navigate social hierarchies. Understanding these dynamics is crucial for creating inclusive and positive virtual communities.

3. The Future of Digital Identity

As VR and AR technologies continue to evolve, the concept of digital identity will become increasingly complex. Future developments may include more realistic and customizable avatars, the integration of biometric data to create accurate representations of users, and the ability to transfer digital identities across different platforms and applications.

These advancements will raise important questions about privacy, ownership, and the ethics of digital self-representation. How much control should users have over their digital identities? What are the implications of using biometric data in virtual environments? Addressing these questions will be essential as we navigate the future of digital identity.

Ethical and Societal Implications: Navigating the New Reality

The transformative potential of VR and AR comes with ethical and societal considerations. As these technologies become more integrated into our lives, it's crucial to address issues related to privacy, accessibility, and the impact on human behavior.

1. Privacy and Data Security

In virtual and augmented environments, users generate vast amounts of data, from personal interactions and biometric information to location data and usage patterns. Protecting this data is paramount to maintaining user trust and ensuring the security of digital experiences.

Developers and platform providers must implement robust security measures and transparent privacy policies. Users should have control over their data, including the ability to manage permissions, understand how their data is used, and opt out of data collection if they choose.

Balancing innovation with privacy protection will be key to the responsible development of VR and AR technologies.

2. Accessibility and Inclusivity

Ensuring that VR and AR experiences are accessible to all users is essential for creating inclusive digital environments. This includes designing interfaces that accommodate different physical abilities, providing options for users with sensory impairments, and ensuring affordability and availability of the technology.

For example, VR platforms can offer customizable controls for users with mobility impairments, or provide audio descriptions and captions for users with visual or hearing impairments. Making these technologies accessible ensures that everyone can benefit from the transformative potential of VR and AR.

3. The Impact on Human Behavior

The immersive nature of VR and AR can influence human behavior in profound ways. While these technologies offer opportunities for positive experiences, they also have the potential for misuse. Concerns include the potential for addiction, the impact of prolonged use on mental and physical health, and the ethical implications of creating hyper-realistic simulations.

Addressing these concerns requires a multifaceted approach, including user education, the development of ethical guidelines, and ongoing research into the effects of VR and AR on human behavior. By understanding and mitigating the risks, we can harness the benefits of these technologies while minimizing potential harms.

The Future of Reality: Infinite Possibilities

As we stand at the threshold of this new frontier, the future of VR and AR is filled with infinite possibilities. These technologies have the potential to transform every aspect of our lives, from how we work and play to how we learn and connect with others.

1. The Integration of VR and AR in Daily Life

In the coming years, we can expect to see VR and AR become more integrated into our daily routines. AR glasses could provide real-time information and navigation, enhance our shopping experiences, and offer immersive educational content. VR could revolutionize remote work, allowing for virtual offices and collaborative environments that feel just as real as physical spaces.

Imagine waking up and donning a pair of AR glasses that provide a personalized overview of your day, with reminders, news updates, and navigation assistance. At work, you might attend virtual meetings in a shared VR office, collaborating with colleagues from around the world as if they were right next to you. After work, you could relax by exploring virtual worlds, attending virtual events, or spending time with friends in digital social spaces.

2. The Evolution of Content and Experiences

The content available for VR and AR will continue to evolve, offering more diverse and sophisticated experiences. Developers will create new genres and formats that leverage the unique capabilities of these technologies, from interactive storytelling and immersive games to virtual tourism and therapeutic applications.

For example, imagine a VR experience that allows you to explore historical events in real-time, making decisions that influence the outcome and learning about history in an immersive and engaging way. Or consider an AR app that enhances your daily jog by overlaying virtual scenery and challenges, turning exercise into a captivating adventure.

3. The Role of AI and Machine Learning

The integration of AI and machine learning with VR and AR will enable more personalized and intelligent experiences. AI-driven characters and environments will respond dynamically to user actions, creating more interactive and engaging virtual worlds. Machine learning algorithms will analyze user behavior to offer tailored content and recommendations, enhancing the overall experience.

For instance, a virtual tutor powered by AI could provide personalized instruction and feedback, adapting to your learning style and progress. In a VR game, AI-driven characters could exhibit realistic behaviors and emotions, creating richer and more immersive narratives. These advancements will push the boundaries of what's possible, creating experiences that are as unique as the individuals who use them.

4. Societal and Cultural Transformation

The widespread adoption of VR and AR will have profound implications for society and culture. These technologies will change how we communicate, learn, work, and entertain ourselves, influencing our values, behaviors, and social structures. As we navigate this transformation, it's essential to consider the broader impact on our lives and communities.

For example, VR and AR could democratize access to education and healthcare, providing high-quality services to underserved populations. They could also foster greater empathy and understanding by allowing users to experience different perspectives and cultures. However, they could also exacerbate existing inequalities and create new ethical dilemmas, such as the potential for surveillance and manipulation.

Navigating these challenges requires a collaborative effort from developers, policymakers, educators, and users. By fostering a culture of innovation and responsibility, we can ensure that VR and AR contribute to a more inclusive, equitable, and humane future.

Conclusion: Embracing the New Reality

The journey into virtual and augmented reality is just beginning. As these technologies continue to evolve and mature, they will redefine our perception of reality, transforming how we live, work, and connect with each other. Embracing this new reality requires a blend of curiosity, creativity, and responsibility, as we explore the infinite possibilities and navigate the challenges that lie ahead.

In this brave new world, the boundaries between the physical and digital realms will blur, creating experiences that are richer, more immersive, and more connected than ever before. Whether it's through the magic of VR, the enhancements of AR, or the seamless integration of both, we are on the cusp of a new era where reality is what we make of it.

Welcome to the future of reality. Welcome to the world of virtual and augmented reality, where imagination knows no bounds, and the only limit is our creativity. As we step into this new frontier, let us do so with a sense of wonder, a spirit of exploration, and a commitment to shaping a better, more connected world for all.

7

Ethical and Societal Implications

ETHICAL AND SOCIETAL IMPLICATIONS

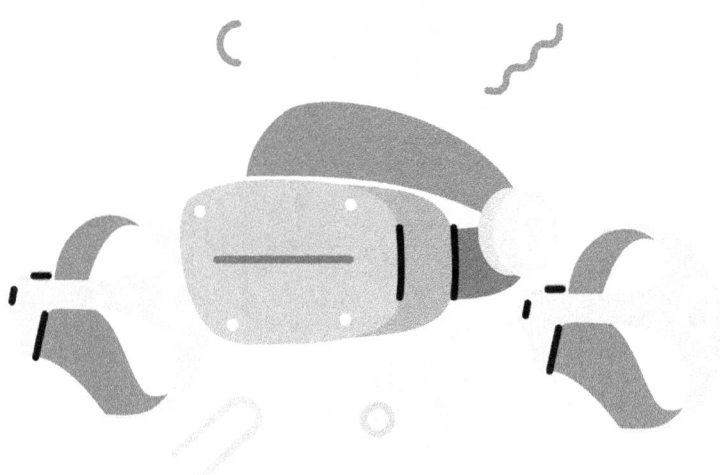

As we journey deeper into the realms of virtual reality (VR) and augmented reality (AR), we find ourselves on the precipice of a new age—one where the boundaries between the physical and the digital blur, and the very fabric of our reality is rewoven. But with this extraordinary power comes a great responsibility. The ethical and societal implications of these technologies are profound and far-reaching. In this chapter, we will explore these implications, examining privacy concerns, addiction and overuse, the digital divide, and the ways we can navigate this brave new world responsibly.

Privacy Concerns: Guarding Our Digital Selves

In the virtual and augmented landscapes we now inhabit, every movement, every interaction, and every choice can be recorded and analyzed. This level of data collection brings with it significant privacy concerns. As we engage more deeply with VR and AR, protecting our digital selves becomes paramount.

1. The Scope of Data Collection

VR and AR technologies collect a vast array of data. From tracking eye movements and recording spatial interactions to capturing biometric data such as heart rate and voice patterns, these systems gather detailed information about our behaviors and preferences. This data can be used to enhance user experiences, tailoring content to individual preferences and improving system performance. However, it also poses risks if misused.

Consider a VR fitness app that monitors your physical activity and provides personalized workout plans. While this data can help you achieve your fitness goals, it also reveals intimate details about your health and lifestyle. If this information were to fall into the wrong hands, it could be used for targeted advertising, discrimination, or even identity theft.

2. Data Security and Breaches

The security of the data collected by VR and AR systems is a major concern. As these technologies become more widespread, they become attractive targets for cyberattacks. A breach in a VR platform could expose sensitive user data, leading to serious consequences.

Developers and platform providers must implement robust security measures to protect user data. This includes encrypting data transmissions, securing servers, and regularly updating software to address vulnerabilities. Users, too, have a role to play in safeguarding their data by using strong passwords, enabling two-factor authentication, and being cautious about the information they share.

3. Consent and Control

One of the fundamental principles of privacy is informed consent. Users should be fully aware of what data is being collected, how it will be used, and who will have access to it. Transparent privacy policies and user-friendly consent mechanisms are essential.

For example, when setting up a VR system, users should be clearly informed about the types of data the system will collect and have the option to opt out of non-essential data collection. Additionally, users should have control over their data, including the ability to delete their information and manage privacy settings.

Addiction and Overuse: Balancing Reality and Virtuality

The immersive nature of VR and AR makes them incredibly engaging, but this very quality can also lead to issues of addiction and overuse. As we spend more time in virtual worlds, finding a balance between digital and physical realities becomes crucial.

1. The Allure of Immersion

The allure of VR and AR lies in their ability to transport us to new worlds and offer experiences that are richer and more interactive than those found in the physical world. This can be both a blessing and a curse. The risk of becoming overly absorbed in virtual environments is real, with potential negative impacts on our physical health, mental well-being, and social relationships.

Consider a gamer who spends hours each day immersed in a VR game, neglecting physical activity, social interactions, and other responsibilities. Over time, this behavior can lead to physical ailments such as eye strain and muscle fatigue, as well as mental health issues like anxiety and depression.

2. Recognizing the Signs of Overuse

Recognizing the signs of VR and AR overuse is the first step toward addressing the issue. Symptoms may include neglecting real-world responsibilities, losing track of time while using VR or AR, and experiencing withdrawal symptoms when unable to access these technologies.

Educators, parents, and mental health professionals should be aware of these signs and work to promote healthy usage patterns. This might involve setting time limits, encouraging breaks, and promoting a balance between virtual and real-world activities.

3. Promoting Healthy Usage

Developers can also play a role in promoting healthy usage by designing features that encourage users to take breaks and maintain a balanced lifestyle. For example, a VR fitness app could include reminders to stay hydrated and take breaks, while a VR game might limit playtime to prevent excessive use.

Users, too, can take proactive steps to manage their VR and AR usage. Setting time limits, creating a designated VR or AR space, and integrating physical activity into virtual experiences are all effective strategies. By fostering a mindful approach to technology use, we can enjoy the benefits of VR and AR without falling prey to their potential downsides.

The Digital Divide: Ensuring Equitable Access

While VR and AR have the potential to transform our lives, not everyone has equal access to these technologies. The digital divide— the gap between those who have access to digital technologies and those who do not—poses a significant challenge to the equitable distribution of the benefits of VR and AR.

1. Barriers to Access

Several factors contribute to the digital divide, including socioeconomic status, geographic location, and physical abilities. VR and AR systems can be expensive, requiring not only the hardware but also compatible devices and reliable internet connections. This puts them out of reach for many individuals and communities, particularly those in low-income or rural areas.

Additionally, physical disabilities can pose barriers to accessing VR and AR. For instance, individuals with limited mobility may find it challenging to use certain VR systems, while those with visual or auditory impairments may struggle to engage with AR content.

2. Bridging the Gap

Addressing the digital divide requires concerted efforts from governments, educational institutions, and technology companies. Initiatives to provide affordable access to VR and AR technologies, as well as training and support, are essential.

For example, schools and libraries can offer VR and AR programs, providing students and community members with access to these technologies. Government grants and subsidies can help lower-income households acquire the necessary hardware. Technology companies can develop more affordable and accessible devices, as well as create inclusive content that caters to diverse needs.

3. Inclusive Design

Inclusive design is a critical component of bridging the digital divide. This approach involves creating technologies that are accessible to everyone, regardless of their abilities or circumstances. For VR and AR, this means designing interfaces that are intuitive and easy to use, providing options for different input methods, and ensuring content is accessible to individuals with disabilities.

For instance, a VR platform might offer voice controls for users with limited mobility or provide visual and auditory enhancements for users with sensory impairments. By prioritizing inclusivity in the design process, we can ensure that the benefits of VR and AR are available to all.

The Impact on Human Behavior: Navigating Ethical Dilemmas

The immersive and interactive nature of VR and AR has profound implications for human behavior. As these technologies become more integrated into our lives, it's essential to navigate the ethical dilemmas they present.

1. The Influence of Virtual Environments

Virtual environments can influence our behavior in significant ways. The Proteus effect, for example, suggests that the appearance and behavior of our avatars can affect how we act in virtual spaces. Users with more attractive or authoritative avatars may exhibit greater confidence and assertiveness, while those with less appealing avatars may behave more submissively.

These influences extend to social interactions, decision-making, and even moral behavior. For instance, studies have shown that individuals may be more likely to engage in unethical behavior in virtual environments where they feel anonymous. Understanding these dynamics is crucial for designing virtual experiences that promote positive behavior and ethical decision-making.

2. The Ethics of Virtual Content

The content of VR and AR experiences also raises ethical questions. What responsibilities do developers have in creating virtual environments? How do we ensure that content is appropriate and does not perpetuate harmful stereotypes or behaviors?

Developers should adhere to ethical guidelines that prioritize user well-being and inclusivity. This includes avoiding content that glorifies violence, discrimination, or other harmful behaviors. It also involves creating diverse and representative characters and narratives that reflect the richness of human experience.

3. The Impact on Mental Health

The psychological impact of VR and AR is another critical consideration. While these technologies can offer therapeutic benefits, such as exposure therapy for phobias or PTSD, they can also pose risks if not used responsibly.

Prolonged immersion in virtual environments can lead to symptoms of dissociation, where individuals feel disconnected from reality. Additionally, the intense stimulation provided by VR and AR can exacerbate conditions like anxiety and depression. Mental health professionals and developers must work together to understand these effects and develop guidelines for safe and beneficial use.

Navigating the Future: Ethical Frameworks and Responsible Innovation

As we continue to explore the potential of VR and AR, establishing ethical frameworks and promoting responsible innovation are essential.

1. Developing Ethical Guidelines

Ethical guidelines for VR and AR should address issues related to privacy, security, inclusivity, and content. These guidelines can be developed through collaboration between technology companies, policymakers, academics, and user communities.

For example, the Immersive Technology Alliance (ITA) has developed a set of principles for ethical VR and AR, which include transparency, user control, and inclusivity. These principles can serve as a foundation for developing more comprehensive guidelines that address the unique challenges of immersive technologies.

2. Promoting Ethical Innovation

Promoting ethical innovation involves creating a culture that values responsibility, transparency, and user well-being. This includes conducting thorough research into the effects of VR and AR, engaging with diverse user communities, and prioritizing ethical considerations in the design and development process.

For instance, companies can establish ethics committees to review new projects and ensure they align with ethical guidelines. They can also invest in research and development to create more inclusive and accessible
technologies, and collaborate with educators and policymakers to promote responsible use.

3. Empowering Users

Empowering users with the knowledge and tools to navigate VR and AR responsibly is also crucial. This involves providing clear information about the risks and benefits of these technologies, as well as offering resources for managing their use.

Educational campaigns can help raise awareness about the potential impacts of VR and AR, while user guides and tutorials can provide practical advice for safe and beneficial use. By empowering users, we can foster a more informed and responsible community.

Conclusion: Embracing Ethical and Responsible Innovation

As we stand on the cusp of a new era in VR and AR, the ethical and societal implications of these technologies are profound and complex. By addressing privacy concerns, promoting healthy usage, bridging the digital divide, and navigating ethical dilemmas, we can harness the transformative power of VR and AR responsibly.

The journey ahead requires collaboration, innovation, and a commitment to ethical principles. By embracing these values, we can create a future where VR and AR enrich our lives, enhance our understanding of the world, and foster deeper connections with one another.

Welcome to the future of VR and AR, where ethical and responsible innovation paves the way for a more inclusive, equitable, and humane world. As we continue to explore the possibilities of these technologies, let us do so with a sense of wonder, a spirit of curiosity, and a dedication to creating a better future for all.

8

Future Directions and Innovations

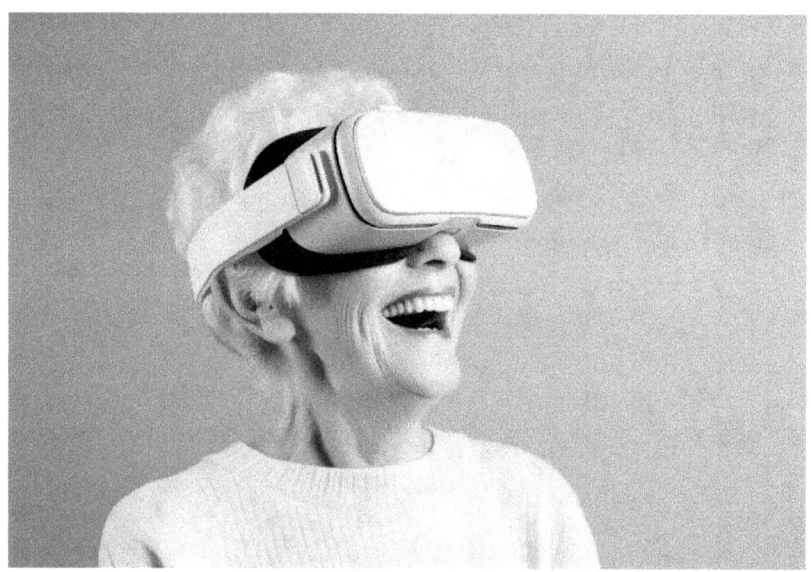

The dawn of virtual reality (VR) and augmented reality (AR) heralds an age of unparalleled innovation and boundless potential. As we stand on the precipice of this new frontier, the horizon is filled with endless possibilities. Imagine a world where the lines between reality and imagination blur, where dreams take shape in vibrant digital landscapes, and where the very fabric of our lives is interwoven with immersive technology. In this chapter, we will explore the future directions and innovations in VR and AR, delving into technological advancements, integration with artificial intelligence (AI), and the convergence of virtual and augmented reality.

Technological Advancements: Pushing the Boundaries of Possibility

The rapid evolution of VR and AR technology is driven by continuous advancements in hardware and software. These innovations are not only enhancing the quality of immersive experiences but also making them more accessible and integrated into our daily lives.

1. Display Technology: Beyond the Screen

One of the most significant areas of advancement is in display technology. Current VR headsets offer high-resolution displays, but the future promises even more impressive visuals. Developments in organic light-emitting diode (OLED) and microLED technology will provide sharper images, higher contrast ratios, and more vibrant colors.

Imagine a VR headset with displays so crisp and clear that the virtual world appears indistinguishable from reality. The advent of ultra-high-definition (UHD) and even 8K displays will bring this vision closer to reality, enhancing the sense of presence and immersion.

2. Haptic Feedback: Feeling the Virtual World

Haptic feedback technology is another crucial area of innovation. While current VR systems can simulate basic tactile sensations, future advancements will allow users to feel textures, temperatures, and even resistance. Haptic gloves and suits equipped with sophisticated sensors and actuators will enable more nuanced interactions with the virtual environment.

Imagine reaching out to touch a virtual object and feeling its rough texture, or experiencing the warmth of a digital sun. These advancements will add a new dimension to VR experiences, making them more realistic and engaging.

3. Motion Tracking and Locomotion: Moving Freely in Virtual Spaces

Improving motion tracking and locomotion is essential for creating seamless VR experiences. Current systems rely on external sensors and controllers, but future advancements will enable more natural and intuitive movement. Inside-out tracking, which uses cameras and sensors embedded in the headset, will provide more accurate and responsive tracking without the need for external devices.

Innovations in locomotion techniques, such as omnidirectional treadmills and motion platforms, will allow users to move freely in virtual spaces. These technologies will enable users to walk, run, and jump in VR, providing a more immersive and interactive experience.

Integration with Artificial Intelligence: Intelligent Virtual Environments

The integration of AI with VR and AR will unlock new possibilities for creating intelligent and responsive virtual environments. AI-driven systems can enhance the realism and interactivity of immersive experiences, making them more personalized and engaging.

1. AI-Powered Characters and NPCs

AI-powered characters and non-player characters (NPCs) will become more lifelike and interactive. These virtual beings will exhibit realistic behaviors, emotions, and responses, creating more dynamic and engaging narratives. Advanced natural language processing (NLP) algorithms will enable NPCs to understand and respond to user input in meaningful ways.

Imagine exploring a virtual world populated with intelligent characters who can engage in complex conversations, remember past interactions, and adapt their behavior based on your actions. These AI-driven NPCs will add depth and richness to VR experiences, making them more immersive and interactive.

2. Personalized Content and Experiences

AI algorithms can analyze user behavior and preferences to deliver personalized content and experiences. Machine learning models can recommend VR and AR experiences tailored to individual interests, ensuring that users always have access to relevant and engaging content.

For example, a VR fitness app could use AI to create customized workout plans based on your fitness level and goals. Similarly, an educational AR app could adapt its content to your learning style and progress, providing a more effective and enjoyable learning experience.

3. Dynamic and Adaptive Environments

AI can also be used to create dynamic and adaptive virtual environments. These environments can change and evolve based on user interactions, creating unique and personalized experiences. Procedural generation algorithms can create vast and diverse virtual landscapes, ensuring that no two experiences are the same.

Imagine exploring a virtual forest that changes with the seasons, or a city that evolves based on your actions and decisions. These dynamic environments will make VR experiences more engaging and replayable, offering endless possibilities for exploration and discovery.

Convergence of Virtual and Augmented Reality: A Unified Future

The convergence of VR and AR, often referred to as mixed reality (MR), represents the next step in the evolution of immersive technology. MR systems combine elements of both VR and AR, creating seamless and integrated experiences that blur the lines between the physical and digital worlds.

FUTURE DIRECTIONS AND INNOVATIONS

1. Mixed Reality Devices: The Best of Both Worlds

Mixed reality devices, such as the Microsoft HoloLens and Magic Leap One, are already paving the way for this convergence. These devices use advanced sensors and cameras to map the physical environment, overlaying digital content that interacts with real-world objects. Future MR devices will become more compact, powerful, and affordable, making them accessible to a broader audience.

Imagine wearing a lightweight pair of MR glasses that seamlessly integrate digital content into your daily life. These glasses could provide real-time information, navigation, and communication, enhancing your interactions with the physical world.

2. Seamless Transition Between Realities

One of the key features of MR is the ability to transition seamlessly between VR and AR experiences. Future MR systems will allow users to move fluidly between fully immersive virtual environments and augmented overlays on the real world. This flexibility will enable new types of experiences that combine the best of both worlds.

For example, you could start your day with an AR-enhanced morning routine, using digital overlays to check the weather, read the news, and plan your schedule. Later, you could dive into a fully immersive VR game or virtual meeting, seamlessly transitioning between realities without changing devices.

3. Collaborative Mixed Reality Experiences

The convergence of VR and AR will also enable new forms of collaboration and social interaction. MR platforms will allow users to work, play, and communicate in shared digital spaces, regardless of their physical location. These collaborative experiences will combine the immersion of VR with the practicality of AR, creating new opportunities for remote work, education, and socialization.

Imagine collaborating with colleagues on a virtual whiteboard, with digital notes and sketches overlaying your real-world workspace. Or participating in a mixed reality social event, where you can interact with friends and family as holograms in your living room. These collaborative MR experiences will make remote interactions more engaging and effective.

The Future of Content Creation: Empowering Creators and Communities

The future of VR and AR will be shaped by the content created for these platforms. Empowering creators and communities to develop innovative and diverse content is essential for the growth and sustainability of the VR and AR ecosystems.

1. Democratizing Content Creation

Advancements in content creation tools and platforms are making it easier for individuals and small teams to create high-quality VR and AR experiences. User-friendly development environments, such as Unity and Unreal Engine, provide powerful tools for building immersive content without requiring extensive technical expertise.

Imagine a future where anyone with a creative vision can develop and share their own VR and AR experiences. Platforms like Oculus VR and Google ARCore are already fostering a vibrant community of developers, artists, and storytellers who are pushing the boundaries of what's possible.

2. Community-Driven Innovation

Community-driven innovation will play a crucial role in the evolution of VR and AR. Open-source projects, collaborative development platforms, and user-generated content will drive the creation of new experiences and applications. By harnessing the collective creativity and expertise of diverse communities, we can accelerate the pace of innovation and ensure that VR and AR continue to evolve in exciting and unexpected ways.

For example, the VRChat community has created thousands of unique worlds and avatars, each contributing to the platform's richness and diversity. Similarly, the ARKit and ARCore developer communities are constantly experimenting with new applications and use cases, driving the evolution of AR technology.

3. Fostering Diversity and Inclusion

Fostering diversity and inclusion in the VR and AR content creation process is essential for ensuring that these technologies reflect and serve the needs of all users. This involves supporting creators from diverse backgrounds, promoting inclusive design practices, and developing content that is representative and respectful of different cultures and experiences.

Initiatives such as Oculus Launch Pad and the XR Access Initiative are working to support underrepresented creators and make VR and AR more inclusive. By prioritizing diversity and inclusion, we can ensure that the future of VR and AR is rich, vibrant, and reflective of the diverse world we live in.

Ethical Considerations and Responsible Innovation: Shaping a Better Future

As we look to the future of VR and AR, it is essential to consider the ethical implications and ensure that we approach innovation responsibly. This involves addressing potential risks, promoting positive societal impacts, and fostering a culture of ethical and responsible development.

1. Addressing Potential Risks

As with any powerful technology, VR and AR pose potential risks that must be addressed. These include issues related to privacy, security, addiction, and the potential for misuse. By proactively identifying and mitigating these risks, we can ensure that VR and AR are used in ways that are safe, ethical, and beneficial.

For example, developers can implement robust data security measures to protect user privacy, design features that promote healthy usage patterns, and establish guidelines for appropriate content and behavior in virtual environments.

2. Promoting Positive Societal Impacts

VR and AR have the potential to drive positive societal impacts, from enhancing education and healthcare to fostering empathy and understanding. By focusing on applications that address societal challenges and improve quality of life, we can harness the power of these technologies for the greater good.

For instance, VR can be used to provide immersive training for medical professionals, improve mental health through therapeutic applications, and create educational experiences that engage and inspire students. AR can enhance accessibility for individuals with disabilities, support environmental conservation through augmented visualizations, and facilitate remote collaboration and communication.

3. Fostering a Culture of Ethical and Responsible Development

Creating a culture of ethical and responsible development involves fostering awareness, education, and collaboration among developers, policymakers, and users. This includes establishing ethical guidelines and best practices, promoting transparency and accountability, and encouraging ongoing dialogue about the societal impacts of VR and AR.

Initiatives such as the XR Safety Initiative (XRSI) and the IEEE Global Initiative on Ethics of Autonomous and Intelligent Systems are working to develop frameworks and resources for ethical VR and AR development. By supporting these efforts and fostering a culture of ethical innovation, we can ensure that VR and AR technologies evolve in ways that are aligned with our values and aspirations.

Conclusion: Embracing the Future with Imagination and Responsibility

As we stand on the threshold of a new era, the future of VR and AR is filled with boundless potential and limitless possibilities. These technologies have the power to transform every aspect of our lives, from how we work and learn to how we connect and play. By embracing innovation with imagination and responsibility, we can shape a future where VR and AR enhance our experiences, enrich our understanding, and foster deeper connections.

The journey ahead is one of exploration and discovery, where the lines between reality and imagination blur, and the possibilities are limited only by our creativity. As we navigate this exciting frontier, let us do so with a sense of wonder, a spirit of curiosity, and a commitment to ethical and responsible development.

Welcome to the future of VR and AR, where the boundaries of reality are redefined, and the dreams of today become the realities of tomorrow. As we embark on this journey together, let us embrace the potential of these transformative technologies and shape a future that is inclusive, equitable, and inspired by the limitless possibilities of human imagination.

9

Conclusion: Embracing the Virtual Frontier

CONCLUSION: EMBRACING THE VIRTUAL FRONTIER

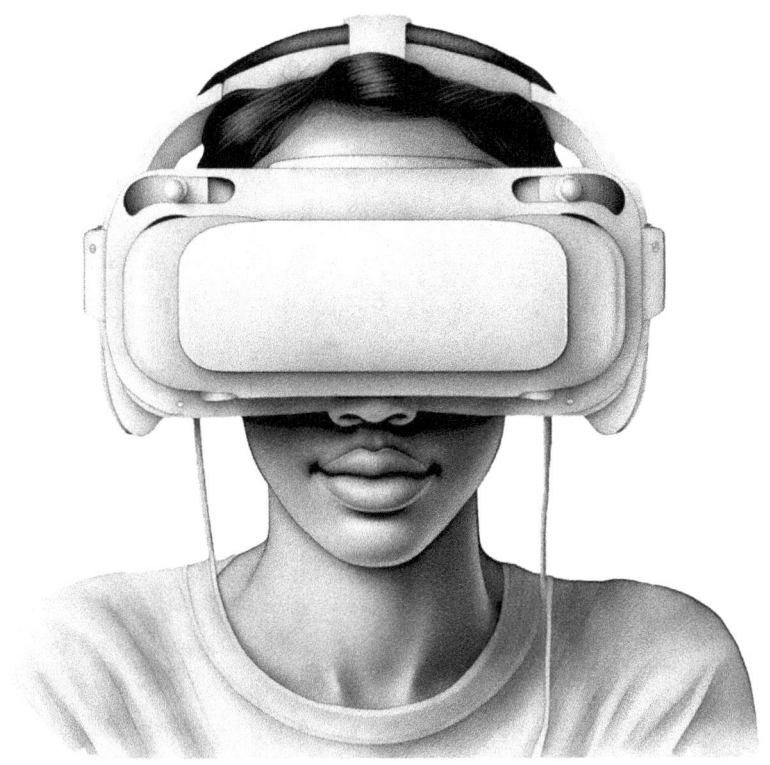

As we reach the end of this journey through the expansive realms of virtual reality (VR) and augmented reality (AR), we find ourselves standing at the edge of a boundless frontier. This book has been an exploration of the myriad ways in which these transformative technologies are reshaping our world. From their historical roots and current applications to their ethical implications and future potential, we have delved deeply into the evolution and impact of VR and AR.

As we conclude this exploration of virtual reality and augmented reality, it is clear that we are on the cusp of a new era. The potential of these technologies to transform our world is vast and exciting. From revolutionizing entertainment and education to advancing healthcare and social interaction, VR and AR offer opportunities that were once the realm of science fiction.

The journey ahead is one of discovery and innovation, where the boundaries of reality are constantly being redefined. As we step into this future, let us do so with a sense of wonder, a spirit of curiosity, and a commitment to ethical and responsible development. By embracing the potential of VR and AR, we can create a world that is richer, more connected, and more imaginative than ever before.

Welcome to the future of reality. Welcome to the world of virtual and augmented reality, where the dreams of today become the realities of tomorrow. As we continue to explore and innovate, let us shape a future that reflects the best of our creativity, compassion, and ingenuity. Together, we can unlock the full potential of these transformative technologies and create a better, more connected world for all.

If you found this book helpful, I'd be very appreciative if you left a favorable review for the book on Amazon!

10

Appendix

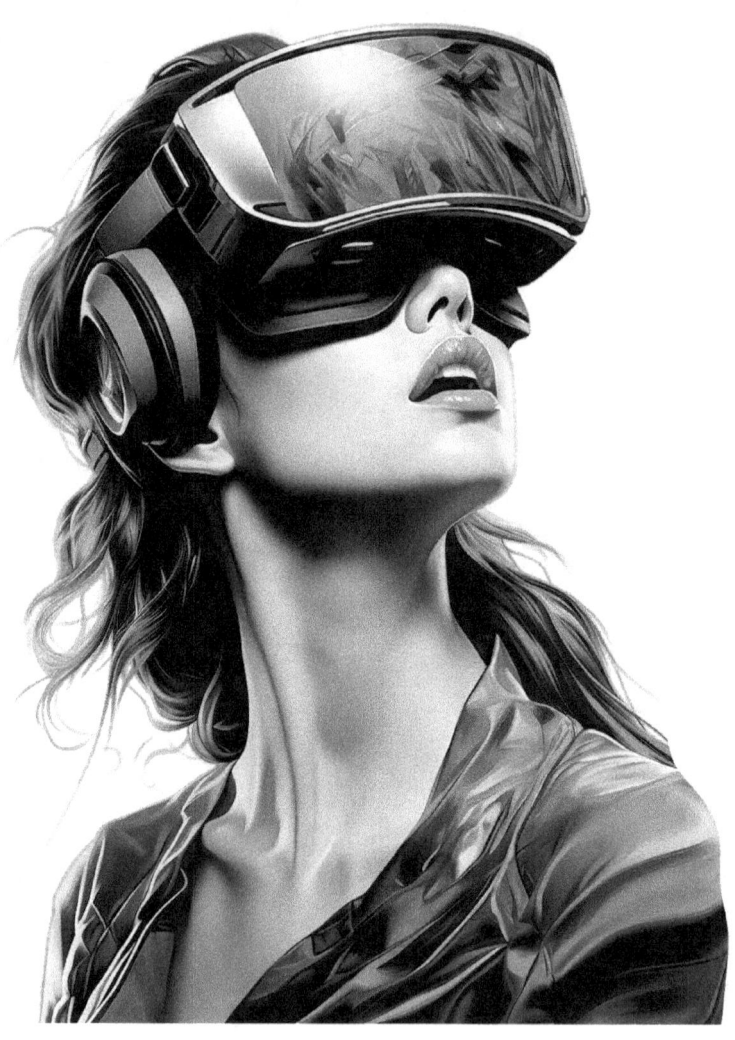

Glossary of Terms

APPENDIX

Augmented Reality (AR): A technology that overlays digital information (such as images, sounds, and text) onto the real-world environment, enhancing the user's perception of reality.

Avatar: A digital representation of a user in a virtual environment, often customizable to reflect the user's preferences and identity.

Haptic Feedback: Technology that simulates the sense of touch by applying forces, vibrations, or motions to the user, enhancing the realism of virtual interactions.

Head-Mounted Display (HMD): A device worn on the head that provides immersive visual and auditory experiences, commonly used in VR applications.

Immersive Environment: A digital or virtual environment that fully engages the user's senses, creating a feeling of presence and immersion.

Mixed Reality (MR): A technology that blends real and virtual worlds, allowing physical and digital objects to coexist and interact in real-time.

Non-Player Character (NPC): A character in a video game or virtual environment controlled by the computer rather than a human player.

Presence: The sensation of being physically present in a non-physical world, often used to describe the immersive experience in VR.

Procedural Generation: A method of creating data algorithmically rather than manually, often used to generate large and complex virtual environments.

Stereoscopic 3D: A technique used to create the illusion of depth in an image by presenting two offset images separately to the left and right eye of the viewer.

Virtual Reality (VR): A technology that creates a fully immersive digital environment, allowing users to interact with and experience a computer-generated world as if it were real.

Key Companies and Developers

Oculus VR: A leading company in the VR industry, known for developing the Oculus Rift headset and later being acquired by Facebook (now Meta).

HTC: A technology company that, in partnership with Valve, developed the HTC Vive VR headset, known for its room-scale VR experiences.

Sony: A major player in the VR market with its PlayStation VR headset, bringing VR experiences to console gamers.

Google: Known for developing AR technologies such as Google Glass and ARCore, as well as VR platforms like Google Cardboard.

Microsoft: Developer of the HoloLens mixed reality headset, which combines AR and VR technologies for enterprise applications.

Magic Leap: A company specializing in AR with its Magic Leap One headset, aimed at creating immersive augmented reality experiences.

Notable VR and AR Applications

Google Expeditions: An educational tool that allows teachers and students to take virtual field trips using VR.

Beat Saber: A popular VR rhythm game where players slice blocks to the beat of music, known for its immersive and engaging gameplay.

Half-Life: Alyx: A critically acclaimed VR game set in the Half-Life universe, praised for its storytelling and interactive mechanics.

VRChat: A social VR platform where users can create avatars, explore virtual worlds, and interact with others in real-time.

Pokémon GO: An AR mobile game that overlays Pokémon onto the real world, encouraging players to explore their surroundings to find and capture virtual creatures.

Microsoft HoloLens: A mixed reality headset used for enterprise applications, including design, education, and remote collaboration.

Notable VR and AR Research and Development Centers

MIT Media Lab: A leading research institution exploring the intersection of technology, media, and society, including advancements in VR and AR.

Stanford Virtual Human Interaction Lab: A research center focused on understanding the implications of VR and AR on human behavior and social interaction.

USC Institute for Creative Technologies: A research institute developing VR and AR technologies for training, education, and therapeutic applications.

University of Illinois at Urbana-Champaign's Beckman Institute: Conducts interdisciplinary research on VR and AR, particularly in the areas of cognitive science and human-computer interaction.

Additional Resources

Books

- Bailenson, Jeremy. *Experience on Demand: What Virtual Reality Is, How It Works, and What It Can Do*. W. W. Norton & Company, 2018.
- Lanier, Jaron. *Dawn of the New Everything: Encounters with Reality and Virtual Reality*. Henry Holt and Co., 2017.

- Murray, Janet. *Hamlet on the Holodeck: The Future of Narrative in Cyberspace*. MIT Press, 1998.

Websites
  - Road to VR: (htttps://www.roadtovr.com)
  - UploadVR: (https://www.uploadvr.com)
  - VRScout: (https://www.vrscout.com)

Organizations
  - XR Association (XRA): An organization dedicated to promoting the responsible development and adoption of VR and AR technologies.
  - Virtual Reality Industry Forum (VRIF): An industry group focused on establishing guidelines and best practices for VR content creation and distribution.
  - Augmented Reality for Enterprise Alliance (AREA): An alliance supporting the adoption of AR in enterprise settings.

Frequently Asked Questions (FAQ)

Q: What is the difference between VR and AR?
A: Virtual reality (VR) creates a fully immersive digital environment, isolating users from the real world. Augmented reality (AR) overlays digital information onto the real world, enhancing the user's perception of their environment.

Q: What equipment do I need to experience VR?
A: To experience VR, you typically need a VR headset, compatible hardware (such as a gaming PC or console), and VR controllers. Some standalone VR headsets, like the Oculus Quest, do not require additional hardware.

APPENDIX

Q: How is VR used in education?

A: VR is used in education to create immersive learning experiences, such as virtual field trips, interactive simulations, and 3D visualizations of complex concepts. These applications enhance engagement and comprehension.

Q: Can VR be used for therapy?

A: Yes, VR is used in therapy to treat conditions like PTSD, anxiety, and phobias. It provides controlled and immersive environments for exposure therapy and can also be used for physical rehabilitation and cognitive therapy.

Q: Are there any health concerns associated with using VR?

A: Some users may experience motion sickness, eye strain, or discomfort from prolonged use of VR. It is important to take breaks, adjust settings for comfort, and use VR responsibly.

Q: What are the ethical considerations of VR and AR?

A: Ethical considerations include privacy and data security, potential addiction and overuse, the digital divide, and the impact on mental health. Addressing these issues is crucial for the responsible development and use of VR and AR technologies.

Q: How do I get started with developing VR or AR content?

A: To start developing VR or AR content, you can use development platforms like Unity or Unreal Engine. These tools provide comprehensive resources and tutorials to help you create immersive experiences. Additionally, joining developer communities and participating in online courses can enhance your skills.

This appendix provides additional context and resources for readers interested in exploring the world of virtual reality and augmented reality further. Whether you are a newcomer to these technologies or an experienced enthusiast, these resources will help you deepen your understanding and engage with the transformative potential of VR and AR.

www.ingramcontent.com/pod-product-compliance
Lightning Source LLC
Chambersburg PA
CBHW050114230526
45470CB00004B/1828